Mr. Wilson
My Life in My Words

Copyright © 2013, Don & Tom Hunt
Profit Proceeds benefit the Mechanicsburg Public Library
ISBN-13: 978-1491070413
ISBN-10: 1491070412

Preface

Almost everyone has a "Mr. Wilson" story. If you had been around Mechanicsburg any length of time, there was probably some incident, action or story you remember about Mr. Wilson's involvement in the school or community. He literally touched the lives of our community as few ever had.

Mr. Wilson first entered my life when I was 10 years old. My family moved into 139 North Main Street, and Mr. Wilson came with the house. Thus, Mr. Wilson and the Hunky Hunt family "adopted" each other. Mr. Wilson watched my brother, Tom, and me grow up, go off to college, marry and raise our own families. He was part of it all but never intrusive and always respectful.

As I grew up with my family and went on to my life in the Air Force, my relationship with Mr. Wilson grew much closer. I think the military experience he had in his early life had a lot to do with that. Even though he loved education and "his kids," there was always a little of that "Sergeant Wilson" that I think he liked remembering. We often talked about what I was doing, and he often reminisced about his Army experiences. He was inquisitive and at ease talking with my wife, Nancy, about where we had been assigned and what the country and people were like. He enjoyed hearing of our travels and loved spending time talking with my children as they were part of "his family."

When I retired from the Air Force in 1989 and returned to Mechanicsburg, Mr. Wilson was still "going strong" after his retirement in 1977. In the early 1990s, Mr. Wilson began to slow down. Being the planner and detail man he was, he sometimes talked with me about "later on:" his preparation and desire regarding long-term care, eventual passing, and funeral arrangements. I was uneasy with these conversations but understood they were important to him.

In 1993, Mr. Wilson decided to go to the Champaign County Nursing Home to manage his health and age difficulties. When he did this, I was his connection, contact, and "military aide" for whatever he needed. Even though his health was failing, his mind was sharp and clear. On a couple of visits, I encouraged him to write about his life.

One day I sat down and penned a three page "outline" for Mr. Wilson of important events in his life. That was the "nudge" that seemed to help in getting his "next project" going. I visited Mr. Wilson, talked with him about his life and gave him the tentative outline and a large yellow legal tablet. He began writing with a number 2 pencil. A few days later, Mr. Wilson gave me 114 single spaced, handwritten, yellow tablet pages of his life. It was the Genesis of what you are about to read.

I had his story typed, but then the writing sat for a while "collecting dust" due to other priorities in my life. After Mr. Wilson passed, I tried working on his writings, but again I became frustrated with the typing, editing, organizing, and all that needed to be done. It just seemed overwhelming. Thus, it went back in the drawer and "collected more dust." Later the project was passed to my brother, Tom, to see if he and I could work to make it happen. Life and circumstances seemed to again hinder us and our progress was slow and limited.

Through the "wonder" of Facebook and the use of modern technology, Tom and Glenn Lewis started communicating about this project, and things started to happen—fast. Glenn, a Mechanicsburg graduate and one of Mr. Wilson's "kids," was the "shaker and mover" in making Mr. Wilson's story a reality.

The production of this book was a team effort. Glenn devoted a great amount of time researching all of Mr. Wilson's writings and several thousand pictures, negatives and slides. He organized, typed, edited and did so much to bring this book to life. Tom was the production manager involved in printing, design, input and planning. I tried to provide what

4

editing input I could, but Glenn's efforts made my job easy. I clarified and provided accuracy to the writing.

Keep in mind that Mr. Wilson's story was written in 1993 by an 81 year old man that grew up in much different times when political correctness was not an issue. This book can't be classified as a pure autobiography as some editing and input were needed. We also included and incorporated some of Mr. Wilson's earlier writings that were on file at the library. There were "Wilson-isms" that needed to be rewritten, explained or clarified. Mr. Wilson wrote just as he spoke in a folksy way, and he sometimes strayed from the subject at hand causing much cutting and pasting of his words in the editing process. Sometimes the syntax or verb tense needed editing.

This is a Mr. Wilson story; more specifically, it is Mr. Wilson's story written in **_his_** own words. It is a fascinating story of his life from beginning to end. I think you will enjoy reading this book and recalling memories from the past.

-Don Hunt

Table of Contents

(The Wilson Homestead)

(Geneva and Dohron)

8

Childhood Years

I, Dohron Clifford Wilson, was born February 8, 1912, in a non-weather boarded, two story log house with a lean-to kitchen. This log house was out in the country around 10 miles from Dexter City in Jackson Township, Noble County, Ohio. It was a tenant house.

My parents were Howard and Daisy (Webber) Wilson. Both were of English decent. Dad was a farmer from a large family. My mother was a one-room school teacher for around eight years before she married Dad in 1910. At that time, all women teachers had to stop teaching when they married.

Around 1915 my parents bought and moved to a 197 acre farm. My sister, Geneva, was born in 1916. (Geneva Wilson McCormick is still living in Mt. Vernon, Ohio. She had no children.)

In 1918 I was six years old and ready to start to the one-room county school which was 2 ½ to 3 miles away. I had to walk this distance each day except on bad, cold days when my mother would put me on a horse behind my teacher, Miss Hazel Lothes, who rode the horse back to school every day and kept it in a farmer's barn near the school. Miss Lothes only taught one year and then got married. Thus, I lost my first "school bus" and had to

9

walk the two or three miles each way until I got through the eighth grade.

Most of the elementary school buildings in Noble County were wood frame buildings painted white with a school bell and a tower on the slate roof. In the center of the one room was a coal stove. Across the front of the room was a real blackboard, now called a chalkboard. Some buildings had only the wall painted black with a chalk tray below. Of course, there was an American flag on the wall above the blackboard with framed pictures of George Washington and Abraham Lincoln on each side. A few school rooms had a world globe.

(The arrow points to Mr. Wilson.)

When I went to the one-room school, the number of students was sometimes quite large, as high as 25 or 30. On one side of the room, the student desks were for the boys and on the other side were for the girls. There was a shelf on each side of the door for lunch pails, and there were hooks for the coats and caps on the wall. We carried drinking water from a neighbor's spring or well for use in the school. There were two outhouses behind the school, one for boys and one for girls.

We would play "Annie Over" (Red Rover) or softball outside with a sock yarn ball. In winter we would bring sleds to school to use at recess.

During the winter of 1919, my whole family was bedridden with the European flu, brought to the US by the returning World War I soldiers. This caused me to be absent from school a big part of that winter.

In the fourth grade, I found that I was interested in history. Our little textbook was mostly about early American men and women. History would affect me the rest of my life.

All my teachers were unmarried ladies. I had Florence Gessel during the 5th-8th grade years. Miss Gessel became my idol, and it was at that time that I decided to try to become a school teacher just like her.

Before and after school, I always had plenty of chores to be done especially during planting and harvest time. In my spare time, I read a lot of books during those years. It seemed that when other boys were out hunting rabbits or other things, I always had work to do or was reading books. I guess my real hobby was reading.

At the end of the 8th grade year, I had to take a test in order to be promoted into high school. I passed the test and was given a diploma issued by the county superintendent. This was my first diploma.

11

When I was ready to begin in the small Jackson Township High School, there were only two of us: a girl and

myself. Because of this, the School Board paid for my transportation to the Dexter City High School while the girl went to Beverly High School. I was lucky because by the time I was a senior, the township had built a new county high school building complete with Industrial Arts and Home Economics Departments. There were only five seniors, including myself, when I graduated from the Dexter City High School in 1931. All five of us had to have a part in the commencement. I gave the class prophecy.

College Education

I had already decided that I wanted to become a school teacher while in the 7th grade but when September 1931 rolled around, the whole nation was in the grip of the 1929 and 1930's Great Depression. Money was scarce and times were difficult. Raw wool was selling for less than half of what it did before 1929.

Since I was the only son, Dad seemed to think I should stay on the farm, but Mom, a former teacher, favored me going to college. I went to Columbus and tried to enter Ohio State University. I discovered they did not offer a two-year teacher course. So I went to Ohio University and found they had plenty of college freshmen in two-year courses. I enrolled and entered O.U. Everything was new and much different than on the farm and Dexter High School. Class competition was much greater, and there were around 4,500 students in the four grades.

I found a room for $3 a week only three blocks from the campus at 32 Congress Street. It was owned by a retired farmer and his wife. It was a good situation. A Greek restaurant was nearby where I could get a full evening meal for 50 cents, including a big-size glass of milk.

I generally went home every second weekend. I had a small cloth-covered case similar to a small suitcase which I carried home with my laundry. I always rode the bus from Athens to Marietta then up Duck Creek into Dexter City. I, then, had to walk the 5 miles to where we lived on Route 330. Generally, I

Dexter City
20 Miles north of
Marietta, OH

13

had to change buses at Marietta. On the return trip, I always had to set my laundry case away from the bus stove because the heat would melt the butter wrapped in wax paper that Mom would always send back.

Dad told me never to try to "thumb" on the highway because it was too dangerous. Dad also told me not to find a job in Athens for pay, because it would take longer to get through the two-year course.

College tuition in 1931 was $50.00 per semester, and student teaching was $8.00 extra. The entire two-year teacher's course cost my parents $800.00 which was an entire, one year's wool check. Dad told me that he expected me to pay back the money from my first year's school salary. (After teaching two years, I tried to pay back the $800, but Dad would not take it. He said that he just told me that because he didn't want me to spend too much money.)

A new idea came out in the 1930's at the very time I entered Ohio University for elementary teacher training. It was to throw out the alphabet and teach first grade pupils by the new sight method. This method of teaching and learning was for the pupil to look at a new word as a "whole word" and get a mental picture forever in his mind. The professors said that the alphabet and the sounds were no good and did not interest the six year old pupil. However, I managed to convince my professors this method of teaching was just "the thing of the time." I received A's in the courses. I would never practice that method in my teaching because my mother, who taught school for 8 years before 1910 and who used the McGuffey Readers, made fun of this new method of teaching reading. She said it would never work, and if I used it in my first school I would be kicked out the first year.

Things went pretty well those two years, and Ohio University granted me a traditional County Education Two-year Teacher's Diploma in 1933.

14

The Board of Trustees of

The Ohio University

on the recommendation of the Faculty, in recognition of the completion of the prescribed course in the

College of Education

has conferred upon

Dohron Clifford Wilson

the degree of

Bachelor of Science in Education

with all the honors, rights, and privileges belonging there to. In witness whereof this diploma has been signed by the duly authorized officers of the University and sealed with its corporate seal given at Athens, state of Ohio, January 31st, year of our Lord 1948, and of the University the 144th.

John C. Baker
President of the University

Secretary of the Board

Evan R. Collins
Dean of the College

15

Getting My First Teaching Position

With my two year teaching diploma, I was ready to get a teaching job in one of the five, one-room schools in Jackson Township. The buildings looked exactly like they were 6 years before when I was in the eighth grade in Townhouse Elementary School.

In those days, it was expected that a teacher candidate would have a personal interview with each of the five School Board Members at their residences. Generally, you were expected to find him somewhere working on his farm, give him your application for any job opening in the five schools, and have a very short outdoor interview. You weren't to let this take too long, because the Board Member didn't like to stop his work in the field. If the farmer was cleaning out the pig pen or sheep house, that's where you had your interview.

After my personal interviews, I was hired at the next formal school board meeting for the Darrah School which was 4 miles from my home. I was hired for $100 per month, but the State School Retirement took out 4% or $4 each month which made the monthly check $96. Since this was in the middle of the Great Depression, the board could only pay teachers, at times, one half or one quarter of each check. Sometimes, there was no check at all. It was not unusual for the board to still be paying for last school year after that teacher was teaching in the next school year. No one ever complained because they knew they would be paid sometime.

Teaching in the One-Room School

When I was a pupil in the one-room school during the 1920's, the parents had to buy all the school textbooks. But in 1933 when I started teaching, the School Board furnished all the books. The School Board also furnished one wooden box (one gross-144 sticks) of blackboard chalk per year

 A boy or girl attending one of the early one-room schools had great advantages over those in the larger consolidated schools. For seven years, he or she sat in the room and listened to those in the other grades go through the sounds and syllables of various primary words being pronounced, read, and recited in their class. Another great advantage was in having the older students help instruct the lower grade students. Often there would not be any pupils in one of the grades at all which would give the teacher more time with the other grades.

In a one-room school, the teacher personally knew the parents of each student because everyone lived close to the school. Everyone in the area took interest in the entire school and not just their own children. It also seemed like those country kids were healthier because the pupil attendance was much better than in the large consolidated elementary schools.

I had no car the first year of teaching, so I walked the 4 miles to and from school each day carrying my lunch box and thermos bottle.

School buses were unheard of then. Most children walked to school. One or two families, who lived more than four miles away, would pay to have their children hauled to school. I had to thaw many first graders' fingers in cold water

17

even though they had gloves on when they walked to school. Students, who had walked the farthest from home, would sit on benches near the red hot stove so they could thaw out and warm up.

The school year was 8 months long. The last day of each year was the last day of April.

The daily bell schedule was:

- 8:30 A.M. warning for children walking.
- 9:00 A.M. school took up.
- 10:45 A.M. ended first recess.
- 1:00 P.M. ended the noon hour.
- 2:45 P.M. ended last recess.

School was always let out at 4:00 P.M.

Reading, Arithmetic, English, Geography, History, Spelling, Health and Writing were the basic subjects taught. The school day was entirely devoted to basic educational instruction. A music teacher came to school one day each week for one hour if she could get through the mud or snow.

The school always had two important programs: one at Christmas (with a tree cut from a nearby field with the farmer's permission) and a last day of school program. The Christmas program was most always taken along with the tree to the nearby country church on Christmas Eve.

A 7th or 8th grade boy was the school janitor who received $5.00 per month or $40.00 for the school year. He would carry one bucket of drinking water from a nearby farmer's hillside spring. Often in hot weather we would run out of water, so the boys or girls would volunteer to go bring another bucket of water. Everyone, including the teacher, drank from the same dipper. We had a rule that if you dipped out more than you could drink, then what was left in the dipper was put in the wash pan beside the water bucket. Anyone who wished, could wash his hands in this pan of waste water. There was a cake of soap in a small dish nearby. I would finally throw this dirty water out before going home each day. On cold winter days the school room would always be cold and ice would form on the water in the bucket.

All five elementary one-room schools in Jackson Township operated directly from the County Superintendent's Office in Caldwell. We sent our monthly reports every 4 weeks to his office. All grade cards went out to the parents every four weeks. At the end of the year, the County Superintendent had to sign them.

In 1933, when I first started to teach, all elementary teachers were given a one-year contract. Then around 1938,

19

the state issued continuing contracts to teachers who had an eight year, professional certificate. I was in the first group of teachers in Ohio to be granted the continuing contract. This new contract procedure ended having to be rehired every year. Because of this, when I was drafted into military service in July 1942, the school board gave me a leave of absence. This meant that a teaching position would be held for me for 30 days after my discharge.

I had completed and enjoyed 9 full years of teaching in the one-room school house in Jackson Township.

Military Service

Dad said he could get me exempt from the service because of our large sheep farm, but I would have to resign from teaching for the duration of the War. I replied that I would go and take my chances because most of our neighbor boys my age were going. If some of them were killed or crippled, then I would always feel guilty.

I took, passed and placed in the A-1 classification on my physical exam. I was in camp for training by the middle of July 1942, only about six months after the attack on Pearl Harbor. I was taken by bus to Fort Hayes in Columbus and then by train to Fort Harrison, Indiana and to a newly built camp near San Antonio, Texas called Camp Swift. I was assigned to Company D, First Battalion, 378th Infantry Regiment, 95th Division. This new 95th Division was one of 66 American infantry divisions to be committed against the Axis Nations during World War II. Company D was made up of 200 men who had been drafted. It was a 30 caliber machine gun company with every man carrying a rifle.

I began as a private on a $50 per month military salary. Drill Sergeants were yelling everywhere. The time was spent with close-order drills, the obstacle course and 10 mile hikes with a 40 pound pack. I did pretty well with the hikes because I was used to that on the farm. However, the rifle range was a different story although I managed to get the General Marksmanship Medal.

21

This training went on for 2 or 3 months. Then one morning the First Sergeant announced the names of those they wanted to take a test for officer's training which required an I.Q. of 110 or more. I took it and had a score of 125. A few days later the word got out that the test's highest scorers would be sent to Fort Benning, Georgia which was only for Infantry Officers' training. I certainly did not want to become responsible for a large group of men in combat.

About a month later, I was promoted to P.F.C. with my salary raised to $52 per month. What a big raise!

One morning at fall-out time, the First Sergeant said Company D needed some help in the mess hall. I fell out and so started my military career in the mess hall. The mess hall crew had a special room in the barracks. Our work schedule was entirely different than that of the regular soldier. There  were two alternating day shifts: one shift serving supper, breakfast and dinner while the other shift could get a pass into town or be free to do what they wished. I liked this kind of a schedule because it gave me more chances to see the country and big cities.

It was not long after I started in the mess hall that I was made a Corporal or in military language, Technician-3, which brought another "big raise" to about $60 per month. This was the same rating and pay as a Special Corporal even though I was classified as second cook.

As time went on, the whole 95th Division moved into Fort Sam Houston very close to San Antonio, Texas. In general this was a much better camp than Camp Swift. The

22

training was much the same only much more intensive. There were a great many 10 mile hikes out to a place called Bullis, located in the wilds of western Texas. There were plenty of chiggers and rattlesnakes. This intensive drill and training went on for some time.

Captain Wight of Company D gave orders to send me to Cook's and Baker's School located at Kelley Field close to San Antonio. I think it was a 6 or 8 week course in a very large mess hall. I came out a certified military cook and baker! I was sent back to Company D and given a promotion to Sergeant or in military language, Technician-4. This brought another raise to $78 per month and a promotion to the position of First Cook. From this time until actual combat in Europe, I did most, if not all, of the baking for Company D. This included cornbread, cake, pies and rolls.

A few weeks later a young G.I. from Kentucky came to me and said, "Sgt. Wilson, your cornbread don't taste as good as Ma's used to at home." Of course, I asked him why it didn't come up to "Ma's" cornbread. He said, "You put too much sugar in yours; it tastes like cake." I thanked him and told him that I had been following the recipe in the military cookbook. The next time we had cornbread, I asked him how he liked it this time. He replied, "Fine! It tastes more like Kentucky cornbread now." I told him that I had put 2 quart dippers less sugar in each 5 gallons of batter.

I made only 2 kinds of cake: chocolate with chocolate icing or yellow with white icing. My berry, cherry, apple and peach pies were all 2 crust type. The boys always liked my rolls which were like small buns.

I really appreciated when the boys made comments about the meals. Coffee was another concern. What made Company D coffee better was that we never put the raw coffee into the 10 gallon kettle of hot water. Instead, we first put the dry coffee into 10 pound muslin sugar sacks and boiled it that way.

The Company's next move was to Camp Polk, Louisiana for a month-long, jungle-like camouflage practice in the bush land in that state. This was where I received the only injury of my entire 3 ½ years in the army. I was directing our mess truck backward into some heavy bushes. One bush caught in the rear wheel and flew up gashing my forehead. I was lucky that it didn't put an eye out. It left a long-time scar.

Another incident that happened at Camp Polk was when my cooks had 200 sandwiches wrapped and stacked on the ground ready to load and take to the boys in the field. Two or three wild razorback hogs got into them and damaged some sandwiches that had to be replaced. I had learned a lesson the hard way!

Company D's next move was a longer distance to Camp Cockscomb, Southern California in the Mohave Desert. This was for desert maneuvers. The climate there was much different than in Louisiana. The temperature got up to 110 or 120 then it would suddenly drop to around 60 degrees soon after sundown. At night it got so cold that each G.I. had to use both army blankets as well as his outer clothing.

Cockscomb was a tent camp with 8 to 10 sleeping cots in each tent. Water was supplied by a water line from the Colorado River many miles away. The blowing sand got into everything including clothing, rifles and food. The cooks had to be very careful while cooking all food on the field stoves. All lids on food had to be closed, even while trying to serve.

I learned that distance in the desert seemed much shorter than it really was. One afternoon I decided to walk to the foothills of the Cockscomb Mountains. But after walking for 2 hours, the mountains seemed as far away as when I had started walking, so I went back to camp.

The eastern return trip by troop train was much farther north: over the Rocky Mountains, through the Great Plains, Northern Indiana and Ohio to Indiantown Gap in Pennsylvania. The mess crew cooked in a box car and the boys rode in railroad coaches. I soon found out that while the

24

train was going through the high Rocky Mountains, it took much longer to cook food than in the field ranges. Water would boil at a much less temperature than 212 degrees because of the high altitude. It even took longer to make coffee.

The box car doors were always open during the day with only a 2x4 plank for a safety rail. For most of the boys, it was the first trip across the entire USA, so they took in the scenery from the box car wishing daylight would last longer. The field stoves were chained fast to the inside of the box car. The G.I.'s were served in  the box car and went back to their passenger car to eat.

The long tour across the US finally ended with a longer, more intensive field training in Indiantown Gap Military Reservation in Pennsylvania. This older permanent reservation had better living conditions except for the mess hall's coal burning cook stoves. It was much more difficult to get these stoves to pass the mess officer's inspections.

Around the first of July, all of Company D was given a 30 day furlough to go home. I had to report back to the "Gap" at the end of the 30 days. The rumor was that my next stop would be the disembarking center at Camp Miles Standish on the east coast.

While at home, I wrote 2 copies of a coded key for Europe and for the South Pacific combat theaters that would get past the censoring officers for my letters back home. I left one copy of each set with my parents and carried a copy of each of the sets in my duffel bag all through combat in Europe. My parents would know exactly what country I was

25

in. An example was: England=horses and Germany=goats. I might say, "Sell my big black horse." My parents would know that I was in England, and the officer would never censor it out.

Well, the 30 day furlough ended, and I reported back to the "Gap." Right away the military began to issue new clothes. I got a metal chain to replace the string cord on my dog tags and a heavy rubber ring that fit over the edge of each of the 2 dog tags to keep them from rattling, a standard procedure for anyone going into combat. The mess crew was even issued new field stoves.

Shortly after returning to Indiantown Gap, I was taken by an army truck to Camp Miles Standish which was an embarkation center. On August 6, 1944, I walked directly from the truck down to the gang plank of the large troop ship, Mariposa. This was a converted luxury liner that had been built before the war to carry tourists to the South Pacific. All the murals on the walls had been covered with plywood. There must have been hundreds of 95th boys on that ship. Some had to sleep under their blankets on the open, top deck.

Company D cooks were lucky because most of us had what had been a very luxurious, one family stateroom. It now had 3 wood deck bunks with a 2 foot wide passageway down the center between the bunk beds. It was so narrow that I had to walk in sideways. The portholes were all painted black and locked closed. Fortunately, the ships ventilation system was excellent. The ship's kitchen crew did all the cooking, and I ate standing up at a narrow counter in the ship's dining room.

The Mariposa left Boston Harbor in blackout in the middle of the night on that first day. The ship's gentle motion seemed to rock me to sleep. When I went up on deck the next morning, there was only the calm ocean. I could feel the big ship gently zigzagging to the right and then to the left, sometimes turning to a 90 degree. This was to evade the many German submarines that were in the North Atlantic Ocean. To my knowledge, no submarine ever was sighted unless the captain of the Mariposa didn't tell.

In the after-part of the night on August 14, 1944, I arrived in the Liverpool, England's harbor, disembarked and transferred silently onto an English passenger train. I rode this train through the central part of England to the very southern part of Southampton.

At daylight, I greatly enjoyed seeing the English countryside. Most of the 95th was quartered in a quite large, permanent English camp in the countryside near Southampton. The object of this was to give both American and English soldiers a chance to operate and drill together.

Here as it was at the "Gap" in Pennsylvania, I found those old dirty, coal burning cook stoves in the English mess halls. The first morning after I had fed supper the night before, two medical officers came into our mess hall and said, "What in the hell did you cooks feed Company D men last night? Ten to twenty of them got intense diarrhea and were running to the latrine half the night!" I said that I knew a lot of our men got passes into Southampton where they went to the English pubs and bought some new kind of English beer. I told him to check with the First Sergeant, who gave out the passes, to see if they were the same as those who got the diarrhea. I told the

27

Sergeant that the cooking utensils in this English mess hall were just as clean as those in the States. The next time the officer came in, he said that I was correct. Our boys just couldn't take their first English beer.

The 95th stayed near Southampton around 2 weeks, and then was taken by landing craft across the English Channel to Normandy Beach on September 14, 1944. The Channel was very rough, and I almost got seasick during the 80 mile trip. I had to walk to shore in shallow water and up the same cliffs as those boys in the original landing back in June. The German pillboxes were now all bombed out, empty and quiet. The battlefront was now a little east of Paris.

I went by truck into the hedge-row country of northwestern France. Most of the Division bivouacked for 2 or 3 weeks while all of our 95th trucks with drivers were taken to haul gasoline and supplies up front to George Patton's Third Army.

I slept in a pup tent on the very damp ground, and cold fog came in from the North Sea. The kitchen was in an open tent. This is where arthritis in my left knee started but never gave me much trouble.

Although it was September, the French hedge-rows contained a lot of very nice, large wild blackberries. Some of Company D boys asked me if I would make them some blackberry pies before the boys had to go into combat. I told them that army cooks were not supposed to feed anything that was not government inspected, and if I did I could find myself as a "Buck Private" in a hurry. I finally agreed. I stayed up and made pies at night. Four to six of the boys would come early the next morning before the officers arrived and take the pies to their pup tents. They brought the empty pans back after dark the next night. Everything went well with this "pie project," and no officer found out. The Company D boys gave me the nickname of Sergeant "Ma" Wilson which I carried until discharge. (In thinking about those berry pies years afterwards, I'm really glad that I took the risk, because that was the last homemade pie some of those boys ever ate before they were killed in action.)

After about 3 weeks when the trucks and drivers came back, Company D left the hedge-row country and moved either by truck or small French box car. I happened to be on one of those small freight cars when it jumped the track in the Paris station. The boys pried it back on with poles. Finally the 95th came together and bivouacked in a large field and woods.

The Company D kitchen had 6 cooks for a 24 hour period in combat. The cooks did not have any clear-cut time for working a shift. I thought there would be arguments as to who would get to sleep, but I don't remember of even one argument. The cooks all worked together as a unit. The boys had been together for so long while in the states that it seemed like we were "brothers," who would quickly protect each other as a unit. Our 6th man, who was the mess sergeant, got "sick" and left the Company. Because I was the ranking first cook, I had to serve as the acting mess sergeant for the remainder of our tour.

One day, I got busy and mixed up four 5 gallon kettles of pancake batter. One of the cooks, who was frying hot cakes, happened to step backward with his mud-covered combat boot into this kettle of batter. I didn't have enough ingredients to make any more batter, so we just skimmed out the mud. The boys never knew the difference. Another time while still in France, the boys had dug a sump (a low space that collects any often-undesirable liquids) in which to throw garbage and mess kit water. Late at night after dumping 30 gallons of this water into the sump, we heard this funny noise. Out crawled a Frenchman who had been looking for pieces of food but instead got a shower of dirty dishwater.

The French people, especially in the country and small villages, treated all Americans like angels from heaven. I remember the Company had permission to put our field kitchen in the end of a barn. The French man and wife invited

29

the cooks to sleep upstairs in the house end of their house/barn building. By this time it was beginning to get pretty cold at night. Their invitation was accepted. The French wife showed us upstairs to two beds, each one with two very thick, red goose feather ticks. We decided that we were to sleep between these two feather ticks, but we found that we had a problem. Every time one person moved, the upper tick would slide off onto the floor. Also, much cold came in between the two ticks. The problem was solved when we put our 4 army blankets cross-wise across the top tick. We gave our French host one or two number 10 cans of meat or vegetables to show our appreciation for their hospitality.

About this time all the boys in the infantry were awarded the Combat Infantryman Badge. This gave us $10 more per month.

Our next move took Company D to Malancourt and into the home of a nice French family where the wife was afraid of airplanes in the night. We would say to her, "Nix-nix, Amerika-Amerika." Our statement would always satisfy her. These really were American bombers going into Germany on a bombing raid, as it was only a few miles to the five heavily fortified forts that protected Metz. I could hear the big guns on the front lines.

It was the first part of November, and the weather had changed to mud, rain, cold and snow. So many boys in Company D had been wounded or killed that all the rear echelon boys were placed in foxholes for 3 days and 3 nights. This included all of the cooks. I was standing in water in the foxhole, because it either snowed or rained the entire 3 days and 3 nights. I was supposed to make the Germans think our regular boys were still on the defense line by firing my rifle.

This plan was successful, because the Germans never attacked our section of the lines. On our last day in these foxholes our Company D, along with the 95th Division, started the attack on the five German forts that protected the big city of Metz. Our men found that all five of these German forts were connected by tunnels. When one fort was taken, it would always be found to be empty of Germans. It took two or more weeks to capture all five of these forts and the city of Metz.

During combat the mess personnel would always cook the food 8 to 10 miles behind the front lines in a German building or house and then take it up to the front lines in a jeep. The jeep had a trailer on which the cooks carried water for the canteens. I would have to go on every trip to the front because of my being acting mess sergeant. About 3 of the other cooks would go to help serve. The entire Company was never served at one time. It was too dangerous to ever have the entire 200 boys together. Also, some had to stay on duty with the machine guns.

The cooks generally would try to serve breakfast around 4 o'clock and be on the way back before it became daylight. The food was kept warm in 5 gallon thermos cans which would steam and cause food to become soggy on the way. The boys often called pancakes, "saddle blankets."

The mess crew was not supposed to wait very long for the second group of boys to come to eat. I remember one

night we were going along the right bank of a river about the size of the Ohio River, and the Germans were holding the left side. We fed the boys in a large country house and got safely back to our kitchen. The next night the boys said, "Ma Wilson, you sure got the mess crew and us out of that farmhouse just in time because in about a half hour the enemy caught on and shelled that farmhouse completely down."

The cooks never had but one minor accident on those trips to the front. Our mess jeep fell into a shell hole, and one of my crew got some black and blue knees.

Generally, the cooks left in the base kitchen would catch 2 or 3 hours sleep while the others were up front. When we came back, the cooks who had slept started to prepare the next meal while we slept. During the hardest of combat we only made one meal per day, the breakfast at 4 A.M. The boys were on C or K rations the rest of the day. We never knew during any 24 hour period when we would receive orders to either move up or retreat.

I remember one night after I had returned from the front. I decided to get a few hours of sleep. A big gun fired from our side to across the street. I thought it was a German tank retaking the city. What really happened was one of our American boys had backed a tank into an alley two doors down and left the hatch lid open. During the night a German shell had come down and fell into the open hatch, setting the tank on fire, which in turn caused the loaded big gun in the tank to fire. It tore a big hole in the house in which all of

32

Company D's duffel bags were stored. I was lucky because mine was not destroyed.

Another time after some very hard fighting, the cooks took chow up to the combat area, and the field officers said that they needed more steel helmets and our mess jeep. They took all our helmets and jeep and said they would pick us up the next day. They didn't come back until the after-part of the next night. So two cooks and I were stuck with an old German man and wife all the next day and most of the next night. The old man and woman were just as much afraid of us as we were of them. We soon burned all their coke balls (German charcoal-like substances) in a small heater stove and froze the remainder of the time.

A month or so after taking Metz, the 95th Division did some very hard fighting in taking Saarbrücken, a large industrial city in Germany. After almost every hard fought battle, the grave crew would stop at our kitchen to get something to eat. They had a truck with a covered bed about 7 feet wide in which they were taking dead men back to a cemetery in France. Bodies were loaded crosswise in the 7 foot bed. There would be 10 to 12 frozen bodies in each load. Each man still had all his combat clothes on except his combat boots. He would then be buried in a single mattress cover.

One night the Company got orders to move up to a German city called Falck, which had just been taken. Company D's kitchen along with some others arrived sometime after midnight. The mess truck was unloaded into a large railroad station, and the crew started to prepare breakfast to be served at 4 o'clock.

While the cooks were getting breakfast, I went out the back door to the loading platform to light the heaters in the three 10 gallon cans of mess kit water. To light them, there was a 3 or 4 foot long heavy wire with a piece of asbestos on the end which I had to soak in gasoline. After this was lit, it was stuck down the vent pipe. I had no more than lit the asbestos when a German sniper started shooting at me from a wood water tower nearby. I dropped the lighted asbestos down to the cement platform and ran inside. As it was ink-black that night, I think that the sniper thought that some dumb G.I. had a lit cigarette. When the light fell to the platform floor, he thought that he had killed his victim. He had fired at least 10 to 12 times into the wall behind me. After this episode, all preparations for breakfast were stopped because the crew realized that something was wrong with our orders to move up.

That same night, the German artillery gave a very intensive shelling aimed at the railroad station that the mess crew was in. We were very scared and ran down into the dark basement without helmets or rifles. None of the shells happened to hit the station, but there were shell holes everywhere in the station yard. Some of the trucks were hit and burned. The train rails were bent up like wire. The next day 4 teenage German boys came to our kitchen and wanted to surrender. One was crying, because he had been told that if he ever surrendered he would be shot by the Americans. These 4 German boys only added to our already too many problems. I could not trust them, so one of the mess crew had to guard them all the time with a loaded rifle. Company D broke through and picked us up in the after-part of the second night.

Now these 4 German boys presented a REAL problem. I had 2 of the cooks take them to our nearby company headquarters. While I was loading to leave, I heard 4 shots up at Company Headquarters.

I told the boys, who came to help load, to do all the loading from the front side of the station because of the sniper in the water tower. So the boys called in a truck with a larger piece of our artillery which shot at the tower until it was ready to fall. The sniper came out yelling, "Amerika Comrade," but he did not live to hit the ground. I did not shed a tear.

Our boys explained what had happened the previous night. The 378 Regiment, including Company D had thought they had found a weak section in the German front lines and advanced too far into this weak section. Then the Germans moved in and surrounded our boys after they were ordered to move up. This was a tactic which was often used by both the Germans and Allies.

The children in France and Germany would be waiting for us with old tin cans in which they wanted us to put any leftover food from our trip to the front. This we did very willingly while in France, Belgium and the Netherlands in return for letting us stay in their homes out of the cold winter weather. We were supposed to dig a sump while in an Allied country, but very little food ever went to the sump except mess kit water with a little food from the boys' mess kits.

In Germany, the children were much more aggressive because they were hungrier. They would fight between each other for any leftover food. The cooks even had to move the 3 field stoves back 2 or 3 feet from a broken out window because they would stand outside and grab hotcakes or pork chops right off the hot griddle, even if it did burn their fingers. One time the mess crew decided to find out just how hungry these German kids were. So we mixed some left over hotcakes into a pile of horse manure just outside the door of the barn part of the house that we cooked in that morning. That did not stop those children. They just sorted out the hotcakes from the horse manure. What they couldn't eat, they carried away in old cans.

After taking Saarbrücken, Company D along with the entire 378th Regiment were taken on a very long trip up into  Belgium for a rest period. The weather was bitter cold and frosty at night. I had not yet been issued arctic overshoes, and I froze 3 or 4 toes on that trip. I was very glad to get back into a friendly country again.

One family let the mess crew put the field kitchen in

35

their new barn and made room in their house for all the cooks. KP's from our company even helped in the kitchen. Our officers said that the cooks needed a rest, too. It was almost like a garrison life in the States. I even did some baking for the boys.

Company D stayed in this rest location 10 or 12 days then moved up into Holland for a short time. Then we came back to the same place we were before in Belgium. From there we soon moved back into Germany and crossed the Rhine River on a pontoon bridge. Then we moved on into Germany to capture the large city of Dortmund. The cooks made the kitchen in a very fine home where we carried the sick old man out into the rain on his mattress and threw his furniture and fine dishes out into the yard.

Hamm was another large city that the 378th Regiment captured. All of this activity took place throughout April of 1945. We were preparing breakfast in a beer hall in Hamm when a German shell came down and exploded in the trees in front. It blew in the door and windows, but breakfast was still fed on time.

After clearing the Ruhr River Pocket and the capture of Hamm, the entire 378th Regiment was sent on a very long move up to Bremen, a German port on the North Sea. We were to help the British Army take Bremen and get the bombed-out seaport back into use as soon as possible.

On May 7, 1945, all Germany surrendered to the Allies. There was no celebration on the front lines, because the troops all knew the war was only half won; there was still the war in the Pacific. The German military men and civilian people seemed to be very happy. On May 8th the 378th Regiment was relieved of duty in the harbor and moved back down to Munster, Germany. While in Munster, we did some occupation duty.

Company D and the kitchen remained at the same place in Münster from May 7th to June 21st, a period of almost 2 months, doing occupational duty. This gave the military time to bring a lot of 18 and 19 year old boys from the States to replace the troops. This was almost as good as garrison life in the states except there were no passes to town .Everything was much easier. All the boys came into the field kitchen in the barn part, and the cooks were permitted to sleep in the house part along with the old German man and his wife. I even made 2 batches of chocolate cake for the boys.

Finally, on June 21st, Company D started on a 2 day move. Some went by truck and some by train back through Belgium and northern France to a large camp named Camp Old Gold. This was just outside the harbor of Le Havre, France, which was only a few miles from Omaha Beach where we had landed September 14, 1944. At Old Gold, we turned in all our field kitchen equipment. Then on June 23, we were trucked to the harbor in Le Havre and were much surprised to see the very same ship, Mariposa, waiting to take us home to the states. The Mariposa moved out of Le Havre harbor on June 23, 1945. This return trip was much more enjoyable than the first trip which took two extra days. This time the big ship sailed in a straight course from Le Havre to Boston, because there were no German submarines to evade. All the portholes were uncovered. There were no blackouts anywhere on the ship. The ship's food was much better, and the general morale of the troops was much higher. After only 6 days, it landed in Boston Harbor on June 29th.

The 95th Division was committed against the German army for 145 days, including one period of 103 consecutive days. During this time, 6,370 officially reported casualties were suffered by the Division. A total of 1,128 of the 95th Division officers and men were killed in action, and 4,783 were wounded. In addition, 391 officers and men were listed as MIA (Missing In Action).

To inflict 6,370 casualties on the 95th Division, the Germans suffered an estimated 47,264 casualties. Of that total, 15,276 Germans were killed or wounded in opposing the

Division, and 31,988 were captured. The German soldiers in Metz called the 95th Division men, "The Iron Men of Metz."

After disembarking from the Mariposa in Boston Harbor, I was taken into a processing station where I was given a 30 day enroute furlough with travel money to my home. This furlough stated that I was ordered to report back for duty at Camp Shelby, Mississippi. I took a bus from Boston to my home near Dexter City, Ohio.

My parents were very surprised to see me because they still thought that I was doing occupation duty in Germany. That 30 day furlough went pretty fast as I hoed corn in the field and harvested hay.

When I reported back to Camp Shelby, there was more intensive rifle and big gun drill. I was issued new clothing, and the mess crew got new field kitchen equipment.

On August 6, 1945, the U.S. dropped the first atomic bomb on Hiroshima. Then on August 9th, they dropped another bomb on Nagasaki. Up to this time, most of our activities had been directed toward the invasion of Japan. The Japanese signed the terms of surrender on September 2, 1945.

Military life went on for the 95th Division until November when the order came to transfer all men with 60 to 75 points to the 44th Infantry Division. This included me. I was in the 44th only one or two weeks and then sent with many others to Camp Atterbury in Indiana for discharge.

When our group arrived, we found that men were being discharged by the hundreds. It was here, while taking the physical for discharge that a very unusual incident happened. While naked as a jaybird, I was given a small glass bottle and sent to a little room to get a urine specimen. All at once the man standing beside me said, "Oh, hell! I'll never get out of this damned army. I can't do a thing." I replied, "Give me your bottle. I have plenty." So two G.I.'s got out of the service on my urine. This was my last "Boy Scout" deed in the army. My Honorable Discharge was dated November 17, 1945.

Military Medals and Ribbons

1. Bronze Star Medal and Ribbon awarded for activities in the battle for Metz

2. Good Conduct Medal and Ribbon awarded for three years without incident

3. Appreciation Medal and Ribbon awarded by the city of Metz in November 1964 to express their appreciation for the liberation of their city in November 1944 by the 95th Division

4. Combat Infantryman's Badge issued to each man who served duty in the Infantry during combat

5. The two Central European Theater of Operation Ribbons with 3 small Bronze Stars which represent the 3 different battle areas in Europe in which I had taken part (Northern France/Normandy, Rhineland including Metz and Saarbrücken, Central Europe and the large Ruhr Pocket/final drive into Germany)

6. The American Campaign Ribbon

7. The World War II Victory Ribbon with one Bronze Star (Victory in Germany)

8. The Germany Occupation Ribbon awarded for 2 months service in occupation of Germany after their surrender, until young replacements could be brought from the US to take our places

9. Ribbon indicating that I was a member of the US Army, one of the 4 branches of the Military

10. Ribbon indicating that I was a member of the US Army in foreign lands

Back to Civilian Life

After arriving back home the second and final time in 1945, I decided to go back to Ohio University and complete a B.S. in Education Degree. So, I notified the Jackson Township Board of Education that I wished to resign from my continuing contract.

Ohio University was still on the semester system, so I didn't have long to wait before the second semester started. This time I decided that I would like to teach in high school because the high school salary schedule was higher than elementary pay scale. I majored in History, Government and Elementary Education with teaching minors in English and Literature, Geography, Geology, Biology, Botany and General Science.

I signed up for the New G.I. Education Bill and was able to use it through my junior and senior year of my B.S. and for half of my Master's Degree. I already had most of my own money for college because I had stayed at home during my 9 years of teaching in the one-room school before the war.

While in my junior and senior years, the classes generally had 45 to 50 students, and most of them were on the G.I. Bill. A big percentage of them really had no business being in college classes.

Starting college in the middle of the school year caused me to be graduated in January 1948. In order not to waste any time, I started on a Master's in Education Degree. I first signed up for the new non-thesis program because I doubted that I was smart enough to ever be granted a Master's Degree. After getting into the graduate-level classes, I found them to be quite small, and only an overall grade average of B had to be maintained. I found the work to not be as difficult as I had thought and left the university in June 1948 with a B.S. Degree and half of a Master's.

The Board of Trustees of

The Ohio University

on the recommendation of the Faculty, in recognition of the completion of the prescribed course in the

Graduate College

has conferred upon

Dohron Clifford Wilson

the degree of

Master of Education

with all the honors, rights, and privileges belonging there to.

In witness whereof this diploma has been signed by the duly authorized officers of the University and sealed with its corporate seal, given at Athens, state of Ohio, August fourteenth, year of our Lord 1954, and of the University the 150th.

John C. Baker
President of the University

Paul R. O'Brien
Secretary of the Board

D. R. Clippinger
Dean of the College

The University's Placement Bureau found me a high school teaching job in Fairfield County. I soon found this position not so desirable because:

- The local superintendent and principal did not get along together very well.
- The grading system was not desirable.
- The discipline was not acceptable.

Through an employment agency in Columbus, I found that there were going to be some positions open for an elementary principal starting in September, 1949.

Sometime in May, 1949, I interviewed with Robert Latta, Mechanicsburg Superintendent, and the superintendents from Ashland City Schools and Piqua City Schools. Each of these superintendents sent me a contract to sign. I selected and signed Mr. Latta's contract for $2,600 the first year, and sent the other two unsigned contracts back to the superintendents.

I selected the Mechanicsburg contract for 3 major reasons:

- I believed every word that Mr. Latta had told me about his plans through the 1950's to accommodate the great number of "War Babies."
- Mr. Latta told me that 95 percent or more of the students would be farm children.
- The school's front lawn looked almost like a college campus.

Actually in my first year, Mr. Latta asked me to act as one of the full-time 6th grade teachers and do all of the principal's reports out of school hours. Thus, Mr. Latta hired me to fill a vacancy in the 6th grade and still hold me with both a teacher's certificate and a   principal's certificate to meet the flood of "War Babies" of the 1950's.

Home Life in Mechanicsburg

I first got a room for around $5.00 per week with Dr. Thompson and his wife on Main Street. After only 2 or 3 weeks, the doctor died and Mrs. Thompson wanted to move upstairs and rent the whole first floor. So I had to move.

I next found a room with Art Longbreak and his wife at 139 North Main Street. At first, I had the upstairs front, south room. I soon had to move to the front, north room  because Mrs. Longbreak said I made too much noise over their bedroom. Within two years, the Longbreaks moved to Columbus, but I stayed in the house.

In 1951 Marion (Hunky) and Martha Hunt and their two boys, Don and Tom, purchased the house. I moved back into the south, front room. I soon found that the Hunt family was very congenial, a well-disciplined family and one that correlated with my own philosophy of living. Soon after the Hunts moved in, my room became almost like an apartment. Hunky said that if I paid for the work and material, I could use the back upstairs hallway. Walter Teets built cabinets and another closet for me.

Hunky was a long-time Captain in the fire department at Patterson Field. He also cooked at his fire station and for its social gatherings. He loved to cook not only at the station but also at home. His specialty was meats of all kinds on the grill and roasts. It was easy and enjoyable for him to cook-up an entire special meal such as at Thanksgiving, Christmas and birthdays. I would always be invited.

Martha Hunt worked for many years as a bookkeeper, secretary, and a part-time beautician at the funeral home.

When the Hunts moved in, Don was in the third grade, and Tom was a few years younger. Both boys were good in school. Don became a good football player in high school, and Tom was always good in mathematics, both in elementary and high school. I've always said from Don's and Tom's high school days that Hunky really knew how to raise two boys. Every summer they took contracts to mow a lot of lawns about town. These two boys always worked together when mowing each lawn. Hunky furnished all the equipment, and the boys got all the money which went into their own bank accounts.

As the years went by, I watched Don and Tom grow up, graduate from high school and go through college. Both boys received college master's degrees and had a family of their own. Don majored in business administration and the military. Don retired after 26 years in the Air Force with a full Colonel rank. Tom majored in mathematics and computer. Tom held a very good position as head of the computer department in a large company.

A major disaster struck all of us at 139 N. Main Street when Hunky passed away in September 1968. It was a very sad time. After his death, I took over the garden at home and mowed the front lawn until Don took over after his retirement from the Air Force.

45

I babysat with Jay, Don's son, many times when he stayed with Martha while Don was in the service. I remember when Jay was only 4 or 5 years old. We had just gotten a new door bell, and he said, "Grandma, we don't need a doorbell because everyone comes right in anyway." Jay's statement concerning the new doorbell was correct because the Hunt house did seem like Grand Central Station for many people traveling across the U.S. or from one state to another. Another time Jay remarked, "Grandma, you need to clean your candles (kerosene lamps)." Also, I remember making a sand box for Jay in the back yard. Jay married and is head of the computer department in a large company in St. Louis. Jay also earned a master's degree.

Getting Settled in Mechanicsburg

Being new to the community, it took some time to settle in and get into my routine. Figuring out my meals was a top priority for this former military cook who had no desire to cook anymore. I would eat cereal in my room in the morning, have lunch at school, and eat my evening meal in town at Tait's, a small restaurant that served good home cooking and was run by Hobe and Dorothy Tait.

I well remember my first evening meal at Tait's. I was eating at the last back table when in came a big-mouthed, short man. He said to Tait loudly, "Tait, have you seen that specimen the board has hired to be our elementary principal?" That was the first and last time that I ever saw Hobe be caught short and not know what to say. Hobe replied, "I guess we'll have to try him out," as a way to keep any more comments from being said while I was there eating. After this man left, I asked Tait who in the world this man was. Tait's reply was, "That's George Kratky. He always has his mouth open, but you'll find him to be one of your best friends." Tait was right; George turned out to be a good friend.

After that episode, I ate at Tait's for many years until Dorothy and Hobe retired. Dorothy always made the most delicious pies, and Hobe always gave me lots of gravy. A full meal at Tait's was always $.98 which included a cup of coffee and a glass of milk.

Two other men that I soon met were about the only people to call me by my first name. I made an early acquaintance with Harry Carter, the high school principal.

47

Harry seemed to adopt me and gave me a lot of advice concerning the school and community. The other person was Donald Sweet. The school year of 1949 - 1950 was Don's very first year of teaching, but he had known Mechanicsburg School and community all his life.

Jake Shelpman was another person I soon thought a lot of because he always told me what he really thought.

Soon after arriving in town, I learned that Mechanicsburg had two very strong assets: The Public Library, and The Goshen Memorial Park. The Library building was built in 1938 and dedicated in 1940. .

The Goshen Memorial Park was first called The Central Ohio Fairgrounds and included 8 central Ohio counties, including Franklin County. It became a beautiful park with many old oak trees and a full-size race track.

Mechanicsburg Exempted Village Schools

August 15, 1949, I arrived in Mechanicsburg in the 1937 Ford all ready to start school. I was employed for 10 months of the year, and the contract was for 2 years. Three elementary teachers (Betty Guy, Phyllis Beath and Cleo Francis) were very helpful. No one on the elementary faculty had more college training than me, so there was no jealousy that I was employed for the principal's position. In fact, I was the first certified elementary principal for Mechanicsburg Schools. The previous leaders had been only regular classroom teachers who were called teaching principals.

There were only two buildings "On the Hill." All of the 375 elementary students were in the old 1894 building except for one section of the 3rd grade. Lucy Moore, Don Moore's mother, had her class in what was later called the East Elementary Building. Her room was down in the basement on a concrete floor. The entire high school, except the Vocational

Arts which was in David Wing's barn, was packed into the 1920 building.

Charles Newman was the custodian of the 1894 Elementary Building. He told me much about the history of the school and town.

In November 1948, the district voted for a new high school building, which was moved into in 1950. It was constructed in the center of the front lawn. The high school Home Economics Department remained in the 1920 building.

An annual event that had been going on a year or two before I came was the Pet Parade. It was an all-school affair held on or near Halloween. The elementary part was mostly the afternoon parade which consisted of a queen, her court, and a little boy crown bearer dressed in a complete little policeman's uniform. The first grade rode a red, white and blue decorated float complete with bunting and a large parade flag. The high school band, in all its glory, led the float followed by the elementary pupils showing off their decorated pets. I always had 4 or 5 students who carried placards on a stick which asked for votes for the school levy. A grand judging of the various pets was held when the students arrived on the football field. Prizes were given to the winners. The queen part of all this followed closely to the homecoming queen activities of the high school. This parade always drew a very large crowd to watch it. The pet parade continued for a few years but was discontinued when the weather two years in a row was cold and windy. The little queen and her court had to be wrapped in army blankets. Thus, the weather was a major factor in doing away with the Pet Parade.

Everything Mr. Latta had told me concerning getting ready for the "War Babies" certainly came true, beginning in the first half of the 1950's. We had 600 elementary pupils. We had 3 rooms of each grade level, except grade one which had 110 pupils in 4 rooms. This made 19 classrooms altogether. For one year there was a temporary wall in Mrs. Guy's room with 2 teachers and 2 separate groups of first graders. We had to have 45 pupils in each of the two sixth grade rooms before the school board would finally decide to hire the 3rd teacher to make three 6th grade rooms.

Then as the "War Babies" kept coming by the dozens, I gradually took over the vacated high school rooms in the 1920 building. I was the person who named the 1920 building, the East Elementary Building, because it became confusing for the 600 students and for the parents trying to find their children in the 2 elementary buildings. I remember this incident as if it

51

took place just yesterday. I was walking in the first floor hall of the East Elementary Building when here comes a 6 year old, first grade boy with his hands in his pockets and walking just as unconcerned as could be. He said, "Mr. Wilson, my room is lost." His thinking was that his room had just up and walked off some place. I said, "Your room is still in the same place it was when you left it, but your problem is that you are in the wrong building. Come with me. I'll take you back to your room." His small world had suddenly become a large and confusing world.

The student population kept growing until the high school was packed into the new 1950 building. Then in 1957, the big gym with 4 new high school classrooms was occupied.

By this time, most of the elementary textbooks, which had been both outdated and in poor physical condition, had been replaced. I had to buy 110 to 115 textbooks in each subject at each grade level.

Superintendent Diley set up a classroom painting schedule where a few classrooms in both the elementary and high school would be painted every summer until they were all painted. Mr. Diley also approached me with another long-term plan to replace all the old student desks. He gave me 3 or 4 school furniture catalogs and told me to select the type of desk that I thought would be best for elementary students. I reported back the next day with a picture of a desk/chair unit priced at $29 per unit. Mr. Diley smiled, which he very seldom did, and said, "Are these the most expensive desks you could find?" I replied, "No, but by the catalog description these desks, like the old one-room school desks, should last a long time. The same desks could be placed in the 4th, 5th, and 6th grade levels because of their wide adjustment range for both desk and chair. Also, the desktops have a varnish finish that can't be cut or scratched with a knife." One concern was that the student chair swiveled which I thought might start squeaking after using a few years.

I asked Mr. Diley to call the company representative and tell him to bring a demonstrator desk. When he came with the sample desk, he asked Mr. Diley how big the desk order might be. Mr. Diley replied that 275 to 300 desks would be purchased over the next few years. Then I asked the representative about any future squeaking of the chair. He said, "As long as you are elementary principal in this school and if any of these chairs start squeaking, just phone me or the company. I'll bring you a new desk free." (That turned out to be a 22 year guarantee, as no squeak ever appeared.)

The real selling point with Mr. Diley was that the adjustment range would permit the teacher to fit the desk to each child in her room, just like fitting a new pair of shoes. The desks were purchased. There was even a wrench put in each teacher's desk to use in the adjustment. A year later, 175 desks were purchased for the 7th and 8th grade rooms.

I liked Superintendent Diley both as a person and school superintendent. When I approached him with some so-called bright idea, he would always give me his attention and look me in the eye. He would say, "Wilson, that will go over like a lead balloon," which would be the end of the conversation. Or his reply might be, "Wilson that is a good idea. Let's try it out." However, if the idea concerned only the elementary school, he would say, "You go ahead with your idea."

Over the years there were some interesting stories that were shared during our administrative meetings. I remember a way back when Superintendent Gant told this story about Bart Saxbe, who at the time was in the 7th or 8th grade. Bart decided to find out how the classroom thermostat worked. So he took it apart and couldn't get it back together again. Superintendent Gant made Bart's dad, Bill, pay for a new thermostat. (A great number of years later after Bart had become a surgeon. I developed a hernia on one side, went to a doctor in Springfield and asked him to operate. His reply was, "Why come to me when Mechanicsburg has Bart Saxbe who is one of the best surgeons in this part of the state?" I was a little hesitant because I remembered the thermostat episode. I thought perhaps he might want to explore inside me and not get all my parts back together. He operated around 1974. He operated on the other side exactly one year later. He did a great job on both operations.)

I got to deal with all kinds of my own problems as a principal. This incident happened in the latter part of the 1950's and concerned a first grade girl from Mrs. Guy's room before the playground had any blacktop.  There was a ring of mud and water around everything on the playground. Soon after the noon hour, a little girl wearing a pretty white imitation fur coat, a bright red toboggan, red gloves, and red overshoes appeared standing in the office door. The unusual part of this picture was that she was holding one red boot with a shoe inside it, and one foot had only a wet, muddy sock on it. I told her to come on in, and we would solve her problem. She said, "When you rang the bell, I tried to jump off the merry-go-round and got stuck in the mud. It pulled one boot and shoe off. Then I stepped, by accident, into the mud again. I don't know what Mom is going to say about this sock." I said, "Don't worry. Take your sock off and put your dry shoe back on without any sock. I will take this sock down in the boys' restroom, wash it out, and put it in the dryer. Come back in 15 or 20 minutes, and you will have a nice dry sock again." (The washer and dryer that I bought for the school sure came in handy over the years.)

Another booby trap in the old one-room schools and also in the 1894 Mechanicsburg School was the old type school desks where the seats raised up. When the seat was up, the crack between the seat and back became wider, and when it was put down the same crack became very narrow. At its widest, it would let a 5 to 10 year old student's foot slide right down through. Then when he or she attempted to pull the foot

and ankle back up and out, it would not come back out, especially if it was a tight fit going down. This would frighten a kid half to death because he thought he was trapped forever. It was impossible to slide the foot out either end of the crack because of the iron hump on the seat and back. What blocked the removal was that the skin on the ankle would bunch up on the underside. The trick for release was to take both the shoe and sock off, get some liquid soap from the restroom and rub it all over the foot and ankle and a few inches above the seat's crack. Then I

55

gradually worked the bunched-up soapy skin, one side at a time, up through the small crack. This same method also helped remove tight rings from girls' and sometimes boys' fingers. Also in the office, I kept a pair of small pliers with a cutter to the very tip, to use for this. Kids' rings were of no value, anyway.

We never did have any very serious eye, ear or throat injuries on the playground. I think this excellent record was brought about mainly because of the reliably of the elementary teachers who used to have to do playground duty, and later by the very reliable, paid playground supervisors. Also, the kids just grew up with the same basic playground rules from kindergarten to 6th grade. They knew exactly what they could and could not play on.

When I came to Mechanicsburg in 1949, there were only the swings and one slide on the playground. We kept adding new pieces of equipment and blacktop through the 28 years I was there. Also, I painted all the equipment for 34 years. In January 1977, the State School Inspector passed our elementary playground with a rating of Excellent.

I retired in July 1977. I had kept wondering what I could get as a gift for the kids that most of them would enjoy. The 2nd grade solved my problem when we stopped at Springfield's Snyder Park after a tour of Shaffer's Bakery. It was hard to get the kids to eat their picnic lunches because they all wanted to spend their time sliding down a new

spiral slide that we found there. The total cost of the slide plus getting it put in was $2,400, which just so happened to be exactly my severance pay in July 1977. Now years later, the kids have been sliding down my severance pay, and I consider that a higher dividend than any other $2,400 that I ever invested.

The Old School Bell

The old bell in the 1894 school building has been observing the activities, trials, and tribulations of the people in the little rural village of Mechanicsburg for a period of over 130 years. It has been perched high up in two different towers or steeples. It began its long and faithful service in 1859 located in the tower of the newly dedicated Methodist church on East Sandusky Street (by Kehl's used car lot). The bell reminded the good people of the village of their religious obligations to themselves, the church and the community.

The bell was molded by The Buckeye Bell Foundry of Cincinnati and cast by G.W. Caffin. It was 28 inches in diameter, made of German bell silver, and weighed approximately 800 pounds. In those days, the casting of a fine bell was supervised by a master craftsman whose duty it was to see that the proper quantity of each of the 3 ingredients were added to make up the total of the molten metal from which the bell was cast.

The old bell served the Methodist people until 1894 when they constructed a new church at the corner of North Main and Race Streets. The Methodists sold the church to the Second Baptist Congregation where it summoned the congregation to church until a fire on June 26, 1936. Sparks, from the burning Culbertson Buggy Works at the corner of East Sandusky and Locust Streets, ignited the church's wood bell tower. When the fire was put out, the bell somehow remained dangling in what was left of the tower. The bell was rescued.

The Second Baptist Congregation felt the bell was too large for their tower, so they negotiated with the school to trade this large bell for the school's smaller bell.

The old bell began the second part of its long career summoning 6-18 year olds to take advantage of a good education. Its familiar sound was heard each morning and at intervals throughout the school day.

So when I arrived at Mechanicsburg Schools in 1949, I found it was my duty to ring the bell. I was afraid that I would be too busy the first few days of school, so I asked Mr. Newman, the custodian, to ring the bell. After that, I rang it in the morning, at noon and the two other recesses until 1967 when a new electric bell was purchased. It still had to substitute many times when the modern bell wouldn't work.

Each time that school would be closed because of ice or snow, I rang the bell at 7:30, so those in town would know there was no school. I also rang the old bell after every home football game victory for the next 28 years.

The old bell was now left in the belfry with the memories and the pigeons but not like a person whose voice became shaky and cracked with advanced age. It was still able to "speak out" with the same soft, mellow and refined tone that was heard the first day it was "born" over 130 years ago.

Mechanicsburg Football and the P.A. System

Soon after coming to Mechanicsburg, I found that I had arrived in a very strong football town. Before the first home game, they asked me to take tickets. I soon found that it was about like taking tickets at the county fair. They were using both driveways, plus people were walking in at the same time. Both school playgrounds, School Street, High Street and North and West Main Streets were filled with cars. I liked taking tickets from the very first game because I found it a way to better get acquainted with the parents and community. This was free work until many years later when workers got paid $5 per night. I always returned my $5 check to the athletic department. I took tickets for the next 32 years, enjoyed every minute, and never missed one single home game.

Back in the 1950's we had larger boys on the football field. We had 1,200 to 1,400 students in grades 1 through 12 and had a great number of parents, grandparents and many community supporters. The teams won a high percentage of their games.

A new football field was badly needed. The Boosters sold $10 bonds to fund the new field. In 1952, the football field was moved to the East, which gave the 500 to 600 elementary students much needed playground space. The football field was graded, leveled and had new field floodlights installed.

I hadn't purchased any of these Booster bonds because I donated my money to improving the elementary playground which was in poor condition and had little equipment. But in 1991 I talked with a man on Main Street who asked me if I knew anything about a $10 bond sold by the Mechanicsburg Boosters. He said that he had found one in his dad's bank box after he died. I explained what the bond was, and then he asked if it was still good. I replied, "No." Many supporters chose never to cash in those bonds.

I furnished a big public address system for the football and basketball games. I also put the P.A. system in my old 1937 Ford and played "Yankee Doodle" and "The Battle of New Orleans" in various parades.

I even had the P.A. system in the Second Baptist Church on East Sandusky Street for the funeral of an 8th grade boy, Steven Hill, who drowned in a farm pond on Wing Road. Mr. Skillman solved my problem of concealing each of the 2 big speakers by placing an arrangement of flowers in front of them.

My P.A. system was used at the Civil War Monument in the cemetery for the local American Legion Memorial Day programs, many outdoor social gatherings and when showing 16mm movies in nearly every church, public building, and some homes in Mechanicsburg.

The Christmas Tree and Decorations

The school Christmas tree and decorations really were a tradition with me. When I was a little boy in the one-room country school, the teacher always had a tree which she sent 2 or 3 of the 7th and 8th grade boys to cut, after she had gotten permission from the farmer.

In 1933 when I came back into these same schools where most of the farm kids did not have much of a Christmas, I decided I would have "An Old Fashion Christmas" for them at school. So each year for 9 years, I had a school tree with room decorations. Everything except the tree was purchased from the Sears Roebuck Catalog and saved each year. The school

62

would always have a Christmas program put on by the students for the parents. Then Santa would come and distribute a gift exchange along with a candy treat furnished by the teacher (Chocolate drops were only eight to ten cents per pound then.). This same tree and program plus a religious part would be taken into the local country church on Christmas Eve.

Santa didn't have any sleigh bells until after 1939 when my Grandmother Wilson's estate was settled. When Dad asked me what I would like to have, that was a very easy question to answer. When I was a small boy, I saw two strands of sleigh bells hanging in her attic closet on the farm. Dad bid and got the bells. I did not get to use these bells only one or two years on Santa, because I was drafted into the war in July 1942.

When I came to Mechanicsburg, I brought the bells and decorations with me and used them to decorate the 1894 Elementary Building for the next 28 years plus 2 years after my retirement. I had a natural pine tree in the 1894 Building from 1949 until 1967 when I had a 15 foot artificial tree custom-made at the factory. I also had a 5 ½ foot, mechanical Santa which talked to the kids by a tape played out of the office and through a small speaker hidden under his whiskers. Also, I had a 40 minute, 16 mm film we always showed the kids. We used to have Christmas carols come out of the fireplace by a tape recording in the office. The elementary music teacher always had the students sing Christmas carols while standing on the wide front stairs in front of the tree. The P.T.A. furnished the treat for each student. Then when the kindergarten was started in 1959, it added about another 80 five year olds. Believe me, this was a mammoth increase over the first Christmas program in 1933 with 16 to 18 total students.

I was younger then and enjoyed every minute of it along with the kids, teachers, and parents. Even now, when my former "kids" (who are up to 60 years of age) are asked what they remember most from their early school days, they almost every time will say, "The Christmas tree, Santa, and the wooden soldier."

Chief Ohito

Chief Ohito was the Shawnee Indian Chief of the Indian village that was on the present site of Mechanicsburg. His statue was sculpted over a male mannequin by Gordon Keith Originals Company in Columbus. The sculptors used Plaster of Paris to bring out the body features of the Indian. The replica stood about 6 feet high in a glass case made by a cabinet maker at Murphy Lumber Company. Ohito had become the emblem or mascot of the entire Mechanicsburg Schools.

The members of all Mechanicsburg School athletic teams were called Indians. I don't believe it had anything to do with Ohito. I have been told that Leon Boutwell, a pure-blooded Indian who lived in Mechanicsburg and worked in the Telegram office, organized a group of young boys into the first football team. People began to call this team Leon Boutwell's Little Indians.

The Wooden Soldier

The elementary kids gave the paddle that I used the name, Wooden Soldier. Really, I didn't have to use it very often. Cracking it flat on the desk making a loud noise like a rifle shot, generally would bring tears. I would say, "How do you think that would feel if it were on the seat of your pants?" I don't think that I ever used the paddle on a class of 80 kindergarten pupils any more than 2 or 3 times in a school year because it could cause a boy or girl to dislike or be afraid of school the rest of his life.

This episode happened not long before I retired. This little 5 year old kindergarten boy had been sent to the office 3 times for causing trouble and not minding the teacher. I decided this was enough, so I gave him 2 whacks. I then followed him to the kindergarten door where he turned around, looked up at me with a very arrogant look and said, "Mr. Wilson you made me pee my pants." I looked at his pants and the evidence was there. So I took him back into the office, gave him a dry pair of pants, told him to go into the storeroom and change. He had beaten me out the first round, and he knew it. So I said, "The next time you are sent in here, I'm going to give you 4 hard whacks which will make you have to pee much more. I'm not going to give you any dry pants. You will just have to go back into the classroom and get on the bus with wet pants. The big boys will laugh at you and call you a baby." He never showed up in the office again.

Fortunately, the Room Mothers kept me supplied with dry clothes, but I never let the children wear the dry school clothes home. I bought a washer and dryer for the school so the children would go home in the same clothes that they had worn to school. I would almost always receive an appreciation note from the mother if she found out that her child had had an accident at school and needed to be cleaned up.

School Patrol

The school safety patrol had been going on before I came to Mechanicsburg in 1949. Eldon Foulk, the teaching principal, had been in charge of it. I think Foulk was a World War II veteran because he had the belts marked with various ranks. I was told that he close-order drilled the boys in the upper hall.

All this was fine except I had had plenty of the military, so I just kept one Captain, one Lieutenant and a substitute for each. Only boys in the 6th grade could hold an

officer's rating. Only the top two boys with the highest grades in each section of the 5th and 6th grades could be on the patrol. I supervised the patrol without pay for many years but later got paid $175 per year.

All patrol equipment was supplied by the AAA office in Urbana. That office treated all the boys in the county, who had served on the safety patrol, to a free movie in the spring.

The school used to have four Coca Cola metal policeman safety signs. Before I staked and locked them down by the streets, I found one out at Bill Hunter's shot full of rifle holes. Another time I found one down on Wing Road under the bridge. I even found one in the Urbana roadside park near where Route 29 intersects with Route 36. Finally, one night the chains were cut, and someone stole the last one.

Finishing My Master's Degree and a Disaster

I worked on the second half of my Master's Degree from 1951 to 1954 while still being a full time principal. I switched from a non-thesis to a thesis-type of degree.

In July 1954, a great disaster struck the Wilson family. My mother was killed by lightning which struck the chimney of the house. When this happened, I had just taken and passed the six hour written Master's test but had not yet taken the oral test on the thesis. This oral test, before four professors, came 3 or 4 weeks after the funeral.

In August 1954, I passed both tests and was awarded a Master in Education (thesis-type) Degree with a total accumulation of 150 semester hours from Ohio University. If I had taken two or three more college courses, I would have received a Superintendent's certificate. It didn't seem to matter as the Mechanicsburg Board offered me the position of Superintendent two different times. I refused both times, because I wanted to stay close to the students in both schools.

The Board of Trustees of

The Ohio University

on the recommendation of the Faculty, in recognition of the completion of the prescribed course in the

Graduate College

has conferred upon

Dohron Clifford Wilson

the degree of

Master of Education

with all the honors, rights, and privileges belonging thereto. In witness whereof this diploma has been signed by the duly authorized officers of the University and sealed with its corporate seal given at Athens, state of Ohio, August fourteenth year of our Lord 1954, and of the University the 150th.

John C. Baker
President of the University

Paul R. O'Brien
Secretary of the Board

D. R. Clippinger
Dean of the College

68

Kindergarten

Sometime during the latter part of the 1958-1959 school year, Mr. Diley asked me what I thought about starting a kindergarten in September of 1959. I replied that during my 150 semester hours of college training nothing much had ever been said about kindergarten, but I was very willing to start one for the good of the kids. I knew that one of the large rooms in the old building would be ideal because kindergarten pupils would need a lot of floor space and not be packed in like our other pupils.

. Mr. Diley realized that there was no kindergarten in any surrounding districts except for Urbana. He said, "You and I have a lot of respect and support from the community, and I have an approach that will perhaps bring us 25 or 30 students the first year. Mechanicsburg will accept area kindergarten students free of any tuition." Mr. Diley said he would bring this up at the next regular board meeting and told me to be sure to be there. The board approved the concept but with a little reluctance.

It would take 60 kindergarten students to get the State of Ohio to fully fund the kindergarten unit. I was concerned that we might not be able to register that many students. Most of the Mechanicsburg parents were very conservative and believed that a kindergarten was an expensive playtime. How would we sell this program?

Mr. Diley said finding the right teacher was the key to the success of the program. I suggested Jane (Wibright) Baker, who had grown up in Mechanicsburg. She was small in stature and just out of college. She accepted the position.

Now, we had the teacher, but no registered kids. We had until the first of September to get information out in our district, and let this information spill out into all surrounding districts without a kindergarten. We invited interested parents to come in and talk to either the Superintendent or me. The only requirement was that the child had to be 5 years old by October 1.

That summer Mr. Diley gave me a budget to buy kindergarten chairs and tables, 3 abacuses, various small educational supplies, and a metal sand table. There was already a piano in the room. I bought 40 sturdy metal chairs with wood seats and 6 long kindergarten tables. I don't remember what the original budget was, but I do remember that I saved $800 of it to have the new kindergarten teacher buy what she thought she needed. However when I asked for those remaining funds later, the board said that the funds had been spent in other places.

The next day after Labor Day came, and I went into the kindergarten room to count heads. We had 39 total students: 24 from our district and 15 from outside of our district. I was well satisfied. The mothers were there with most of those 39. I welcomed all the little 5 year olds and told them that no matter where their home school was, each of them was very important to us at Mechanicsburg Schools. I told them that if they ever had any problems or got lost to just come to the elementary office next door.

The following school year we had 48 kindergarten students with 28 from our district and 20 from outside of our district.

In the 3rd year of kindergarten we met the state quota of 60 total students. Mr. Diley's and the board's kindergarten plan had worked

I'll have to admit that I experienced one mistake in setting up the kindergarten room. I filled the metal sand table half full of sand. In 2 or 3 weeks, the kids had most of the sand out of the box and all over the floor. I soon learned to fill it less than a quarter of the way full.

Elementary School Art Department

In the late 1950's, Sproat Slasor was employed as a half-time elementary art teacher, a part-time regular classroom teacher and a 5th and 6th grade basketball coach. In just a couple years, he became a full-time art instructor for both the elementary and high school. Soon our school was giving the Urbana City Schools strong competition in art at the county fair.

Our elementary art department remained strong and held an annual art show each spring.

Physical Improvements in the 1950's

New fire escapes were put on the 1894 Building in 1950 as specified by the levy for the new 1950 high school building program.

In 1957 when the new large gymnasium and stage was constructed, the elementary school gained:

- A new heating system to replace the 5 old original coal-fed furnaces in the 1894 building.
- More access to the little gymnasium in the 1939 building.
- A much larger school kitchen and cafeteria in the old gymnasium.

Gymnasium Seats

For three years after the 1957 gymnasium/auditorium was constructed, the spectators sat on the edge of the cement. I had a bright idea, and asked Mr. Diley what he thought about having an all school project to collect sales tax stamps, redeem them and use the money to buy chairs for the new gym. I told him that a large number of students, parents, grandparents; and the general public had watched a basketball game while sitting on the cold concrete steps. Times were good, and people were buying lots of things. This time he did not say my idea would "Go over like a lead balloon." He fell for it hook, line and sinker. He even had his wife and P.T.A. members come up every Friday to count the stamps and tie them in packages. This project went on for a little over a year. We soon had enough money to purchase all the nice gymnasium/auditorium chairs.

Death of My Father and Travel in the States

My father died in March of 1967. My sister, Geneva, and I had a sale to settle up our parents' estate. So the next summer, I began my traveling.

My four week trip by car took me through the southwestern and western states. On my way out west, I traveled through Indiana, Illinois, Mississippi, Oklahoma, Texas, New Mexico, Arizona, Nevada, and California. I really enjoyed seeing the Painted Desert, the Petrified Forest, and the large Grand Canyon. Boulder Dam (Hoover Dam) was quite a sight since it was the highest dam in the world at 727 feet high. In California I visited Disneyland and saw the sequoia trees in Yosemite National Park.

On my trip back east, I traveled through Nevada, Wyoming, South Dakota, Iowa, Missouri, and Illinois. I went to the Great Salt Lake where I bottled up 2 gallons of Salt Lake water for an experiment to show the school kids how a fresh egg would float on top of the Salt Lake water and sink to the bottom in fresh water. I visited the famous Mormon Church, Yellowstone National Park with Old Faithful and the black bears, the Bad Lands, and the Corn Palace. I saw the bronze statues of Tom Sawyer and Huckleberry Finn and Lincoln's home in Springfield, Illinois. Then I took Route 40 back towards home.

During the summer of 1969, I took another car trip through the southeastern and eastern states. I traveled across

Kentucky, Tennessee, Arkansas, Louisiana, Mississippi, Alabama, and Florida. I visited Lincoln's birthplace cabin, Stephen Foster's My Old Kentucky Home State Park, Nashville, and 2 or 3 large Confederate and Union cemeteries. I toured a World War II battleship, a submarine, the Everglades, Kennedy Space Center and 3 old Spanish forts.

Next I traveled north through Georgia, South and North Carolina, Virginia, Maryland, Pennsylvania, New York, and Massachusetts.

I drove on the Great Smokey Mountain Highway to Old Virginia and Richmond. I stopped on the way at

Appomattox where Lee surrendered to General Grant in 1865 and at Yorktown where Cornwallis surrendered to Washington in 1781. I visited Mount Vernon, the Washington D.C. sites including Arlington Cemetery and spent part of one afternoon on the Gettysburg Battle

Field. I viewed all of the War for Independence sites- the Liberty Bell, Independence Hall and Benjamin Franklin's grave. I walked part way up the Statue of Liberty, visited Franklin Roosevelt's home and toured John D. Rockefeller's mansion.

Boston was full of early American History. I was in the Old North Church where Paul Revere hung the lanterns to let the Minute Men know whether the British were coming by land or by sea. I saw where Revere took his famous midnight ride to warn the citizens of Boston. I visited Bunker Hill Monument where the Minutemen whipped the British Redcoats. I enjoyed touring Boston Harbor where the Boston Tea Party took place and where an old sailing war vessel from the War of 1812, The Constitution (Old Ironsides), was anchored.

I took the New York State Expressway to Albany and Niagara Falls, visiting both the American and Canadian Falls. From there, I was homeward bound.

Foreign Tours

My six foreign tours were purchased and planned by Lewis Travel Agency in Columbus for the summers of 1970 through 1975. The one lump sum cost included all air/land/water travel, passport, visas, English-speaking guides, and any required immunizations. I generally started my trip with $1,000 to $1,200 in traveler's checks. I wore a money belt day and night and never had one penny stolen anywhere.

My 1970 tour lasted 29 days. I first met my tour guide at Kennedy Airport in New York City. He took care of getting my one piece of luggage checked in and prepared me for the long trip ahead.

I arrived in London airport, and visited St. Paul's Cathedral, Westminster Abbey (where most of the kings and queens of England are entombed), the king's palace, the king's summer palace (outside London), the Houses of Parliament, Big Ben (the clock), London Bridge, some English countryside, and an old medieval prison.

The next day I flew to Paris where I saw the Eiffel Tower, the Arc de Triomphe, the grave of France's Unknown Soldier, the Louvre (one of the largest museums in the world), Parade Street of Paris, the Tomb of Napoleon I, and Notre Dame Cathedral.

Next, I went by tour bus up to Belgium, the Netherlands (where a great many tulips were grown and then bulbs sold all over the world), West Germany and then Zurich, Switzerland (which was a city in the Alps). I took a cog railcar to the top of a large mountain peak. Switzerland was one of the most beautiful countries that I ever visited. In Zurich, I purchased 3 very beautiful, small alarm clocks which played music.

Next, I traveled by bus through the Brenner Pass of the Alps in western Austria to Northern Italy. In Venice, a very old city built on the water and slowly sinking each year, I took a gondola boat ride on the Grand Canal and visited Saint Mark's Cathedral. There were no streets in Venice, only canals. It was a very dirty place because all their garbage was thrown into the canals for the tide to carry out.

A bus took me through lots of grape and olive tree farms to Florence (a city known for its very fine art gallery and Michelangelo's statue of David) and down through the countryside to Rome. I walked all over the ancient coliseum where Romans used to have men and bull fights. I viewed other ancient Roman ruins and Saint Peter's Church in Vatican City.

My trip continued to Naples and Pompeii (the city buried on August 24, 79 A.D. by ashes blown from the Mt. Vesuvius volcano). Then I boarded a steamship for Athens, Greece. While on this ship, I had my first attack of traveler's complaint (intense diarrhea). I was lucky because it was only a one day ship ride to Athens, and I was okay by the time we arrived and did not miss anything.

I had a big time visiting those Old Greek ruins of The Parthenon and the Acropolis two different times-once with the tour group and the next day on my own. Athens was the end of the tour. I traveled by air to Paris, changed planes, and then flew on home.

My next 30 day foreign tour was July and August of 1971 to Japan, Hong Kong, the Philippine Islands, Bangkok, Singapore, and the Hawaiian Islands. I flew from Los Angeles to Tokyo and toured the many Buddhist temples and shrines. There were many giant bronze statutes of Buddha and a lot of small places in which to pray along the highways.

The Japanese were especially polite. They ate mostly rice and fish. In the rural areas, they ate with chopsticks while sitting on cushions on the floor. Everything was very clean, even out in the country. The average farm consisted of 2½ acres with half of the farm land being used for growing rice. The countryside was very beautiful with its tea gardens. The Japanese were very artistic in flower arrangement, rock gardens, and pruning shrubs to look like animal shapes. I did not get to see Mt. Fuji, their sacred mountain, because there was too much fog.

Although I was there the latter part of July, I saw many elementary school groups with teachers visiting the shrines. The girls were wearing dark blue skirts with white middy blouses. The boys were wearing dark blue suits with white shirts. They looked like "live dolls." Their discipline was excellent.

I traveled on the famous Bullet Train which traveled at 125 to 157 mph from Tokyo through Kyoto to Osaka.

Japan was famous for its Geisha Girls who were singing, dancing, and entertainment girls. They wore a nice kimono with an Obi, and had black hair decorated with a flower. The Geisha girl's facial make-up was a snow-white chalk color. The tour guide had employed a Geisha Girl to perform for me while I enjoyed Japanese tea. The formal tea cups were very small, and the tea was strong enough to walk.

I boarded a plane which took me from Osaka to Taiwan, sometimes called Formosa. The people there were Chinese. That evening the tour guide provided me with a Chinese dinner which I ate with chopsticks. This certainly was an experience!

The next morning I flew to Hong Kong which belonged to England but would soon be turned back to the Chinese. Hong Kong and Kowloon (across the bay) were both cities where all purchases were duty-free. I purchased a Chinese wrist watch in Kowloon.

My next plane trip took me from Hong Kong down to Manila, in the Philippine Islands. The guide took me on a tour of the city. One outstanding site was the old Spanish fort or prison where the Japanese kept Philippine and American Soldiers. When the tide came in, the prison flooded and the prisoners were drowned.

The next day I flew over the South China Sea and South Vietnam to Bangkok, Thailand. This was a dirty city in which I saw lots of Buddhist Temples and filthy food markets. Their stores and markets were fairly cheap. I saw some rubber tree plantations.

From there I had a flight down to Singapore City, an island at the very tip of the Malaysian Peninsula. Most of the people were Chinese. The city had one of the main gateway harbors in the world where 40,000 ships entered and left each year. Raw rubber and spices were the chief cargo.

This was the end of the regular tour, but I had planned an additional 3 day tour of the Hawaiian Islands. So when the plane landed in Honolulu to refuel, I got off and was met by a local guide who put an orchid lei around my neck. Then he took me to my hotel facing Waikiki Beach.

The next day I took an all-day tour and saw Punch Bowl National Cemetery. This was located in an old volcano on top of Diamond Head Mountain which was a half-way landmark for troops going to the South Pacific in World War II. Thousands of soldiers killed in both World War II and the Korean War were buried in this cemetery. I found the grave of Ernie (Ernest) Pyle, a syndicated World War II news reporter who was killed by a machine gunner in Okinawa in 1945. Ernie reported mostly from the European Theater before going to the South Pacific.

Next I toured Honolulu, King Kamehameha II's Palace, the new Capitol building, and Waikiki Beach. I ate poi for lunch which was a starchy food made from the native taro plant. The natives ate it with their fingers. It was something like our tapioca. In the afternoon the guide took me on a complete tour around the island. I saw many pineapple fields and a

Dole Pineapple Plant where one-third of all the pineapples in the world were grown. Then I visited three sugar cane plantations and saw the process of making cane sugar. Sugar cane was the island's most important crop with pineapples being the second largest crop.

On the north side of the island, I saw a black sand beach naturally made of finely powdered lava. I traveled through a mountain pass or valley filled with giant ferns and rich green vegetation to Honolulu. That evening, I attended the Kodak Show which was an open-air show of native dancing and performing.

The next forenoon the guide and I went with a tour group on a motor boat trip to Pearl Harbor, which was attacked by the Japanese on December 7, 1941. I had a tour of the U.S.S. Arizona Memorial and the harbor. That same afternoon, I boarded a plane for the long flight back to Los Angeles then on to Columbus.

My 1972 trip was to Africa. I flew to Paris then on to Addis Ababa, Ethiopia in Eastern Africa. Less than 100 years ago, Africa was called The Dark Continent, but I found some parts of it to be almost as modern as the U.S.A.

Most of the big game reservations were located from Ethiopia on south to Cape Town on the Cape of Good Hope. Each of these game reservations was owned and operated by the county in which it was located. No tourist was ever permitted out of the Land Rover in which he was riding. The Land Rover had an open top that permitted standing up and taking pictures. The vehicle had four wheel drive because all the roads were dirt and also for a quick get-a-way in case of stampeding or mad animals.

On the safari, I saw lions, giraffes, leopards, impalas, gnus (very ugly), flamingos, okapis, many elephants, baboons, apes, chimpanzees, gorillas, zebra, cheetahs, gazelles, porcupines, spotted hyenas, small monkeys, wild donkeys, rhinoceroses, and hippopotami (living in water holes). My two

favorite animals were the giraffes and zebras. The giraffe had pretty brown eyes and ran 35 to 40 miles per hour. The zebra had either black or brown stripes. I saw most of the wild animals in the grasslands or near a very weird looking tree called the baobab tree. It looked like a tree growing upside down with the roots sticking up from a very thick trunk.

The only souvenir that I didn't buy, which afterward I wished that I had, was a zebra skin. The kids would have liked it, but the skins were selling for around $200. So I wound up with only a zebra tail skin.

Other highlights on the game reservations were Victoria Falls on the Zambezi River and Mt. Kilimanjaro. At the Kenyan reservation I stayed one night in the Tree Tops Motel where I could take pictures of wild animals coming to a nearby watering hole to drink.

I visited Johannesburg to see a gold mine, and Kimberley to view an old diamond mine. Also, I toured Cape Town and the Cape of Good Hope before returning to Addis Ababa, in Ethiopia. There I boarded a plane for Cairo, Egypt.

A driver from a local tour agency met me at the airport  and took me to my hotel in Cairo. The next morning he took me out to see the Great Pyramids and Sphinx. No concrete was used to build the pyramids, but a razor blade would not fit between the building blocks. The Sphinx was carved from a solid rock.

Muslim was the official religion of Egypt. The guide toured me through three large Muslim Mosques and the Cairo National Museum. One room was filled with Egyptian mummies displayed in their coffins. Many of these artifacts were found in the tombs of the pharaohs in the Valley of the Kings. The Egyptians' strong belief of a life after death caused them to place about everything they owned in the tombs. The gold mask found over King Tut's face along with his mummy was in this museum. This was one of the most interesting museums that I had ever visited.

The next morning I boarded a small plane for a tour up the Nile and the Nile River Valley. I stopped at the Karnak ruins of King Ramses II's temple with its 78 foot high columns in the main hall which were still standing. The Great Hall was the largest columned hall ever built by man.

My next stop was at Thebes and the Valley of the Kings. This valley was on the west side of the river. There in the cliffs were the tombs of a great number of ancient kings and queens of Egypt. King Tut's tomb was the first tomb ever opened that grave robbers had not found.

I traveled to Aswan and toured the Aswan High Dam. I flew up the river over Lake Nasser to Abu Simbel which was a large temple honoring Pharaoh Ramses II. This temple, with the help of U.S. and Russia, was taken apart and moved to higher ground just above the original site to keep it out of the rising waters of the new Aswan Dam. The guide took me out on Lake Nasser to the top of an ancient ruin that was already half submerged and showed how the big building stones were locked together with bronze lock pins.

From Aswan I went back to Abu Simbel and flew back to Cairo. The next morning, I boarded a plane for home.

My 1973 trip had me touring most of the countries of South America, the Galapagos Islands, San Blas Islands, and the Panama Canal. I flew From Miami to Quito, Ecuador. The next morning I woke up with travelers complaint and had to miss the forenoon tour of Quito.

From Quito, I flew the 650 mile distance to the Galapagos Islands and stayed overnight. I saw some giant turtles (500 pounds or more), iguanas, a four foot horny lizard-like animal, blue-footed boobies, a few penguins and thousands of scarlet crabs.

I flew back to Quito and caught a plane for Panama where I took an air tour of the Panama Canal. The next stop was the San Blas Islands just off the northern shore of Panama. The San Blas Indians were very artistic in that they made souvenir clothes with designs made by sewing together

many layers of cloth. I purchased quite a few of these pieces of art.

Next the tour went to Bogota, Colombia then down to Lima, Peru. Peru was a country very rich in artifacts and ruins related to the Inca Indians and Spanish history.

Machu Picchu, the ancient Incan Indian ruins, stood on an 8,000 foot mountain about 50 miles from Cusco, Peru. I had to go up the mountain to the ruins on a small-sized train from Cusco and then on a small bus traveling a narrow road filled with many horseshoe curves. It was a very interesting ruins and well worth the time it took to get there.

I took a bus back to Lima, stayed all night, and then took a small motor boat down the Amazon River through the jungle as far as Manaus. This sure was an adventure! There were big snakes, monkeys, and bright feathered birds in the trees along the bank. The guide stopped the motor and let the boat quietly float so as to not scare the wild animals away. I was afraid that the giant mosquitoes might bite and give me malaria fever or something.

Along the way the boat would stop at landings and the Amazon Indians would be there to sell their native-made souvenirs. Good sized ships or boats would travel up the Amazon River as far as Manaus so I got to see them loading raw rubber and other jungle products for export.

I took a small plane to Brazil where I saw the statue of Christ the

Redeemer at the entrance to the harbor. The next morning the guide took me out to this 100 foot statue on Corcovado Mountain, sometimes called Sugar Loaf. This mountain rose 2,310 feet above the city. I walked up a great number of steps and then took a cable car the remainder of the way to the statue. It was worth the difficult climb.

Next I saw the very scenic Iguazu Falls, Buenos Aires, many large cattle ranches, and a glacier which was at a summer resort town high in the Andes Mountains. When the plane arrived, there was 6 to 8 inches of snow on the runway. I stayed at the resort that night then flew on to Valparaiso, Chile which was not many miles from the Antarctic Peninsula.

Finally, I flew home. This trip was not quite as interesting to me as the other trips I had taken. It irritated me that the planes were never on schedule.

My 1974 trip was a 32 day tour of Australia, New Zealand, New Guinea, the Fiji Islands and Tahiti. After the long 14 hour plane trip to Auckland, I was ready for a bed. The next morning I took a city tour and found all the traffic kept to the left just as it was in England. In the afternoon I rode on a bus to Rotorua where there were many hot springs scattered over a large area. The motel was heated with the hot water from one of these springs. That evening I saw a program put on by the Maoris who are known for their great skill in wood carving and weaving.

The next forenoon I had a bus tour down the full length of New Zealand. The countryside was very beautiful with the year-round green grass. The farms, called paddocks, had sheep and cows that grazed year-round because of the mild climate. The guide told me that all the sheep and cows were very healthy and that New Zealand didn't permit any live animals to be imported from other countries.

I flew from Wellington to Sydney, Australia where I toured the Sydney Bridge and the famous Sydney Opera House. I learned that the Aborigines were the original natives. I saw some Aboriginal art on rocks and tree bark. These black

people were very frightening to look at. One Saturday evening when I was walking alone on a street in Sydney, I passed an English pub. A big black Aborigine came out and said, "Come in and have a drink with us." I kept walking but said very politely, "No thanks. I have to get back to my hotel."

I enjoyed seeing the friendly little koala, the platypus (which laid eggs and had duck-like, webbed feet and a bill), the dingo (a wild dog that killed sheep), 2 kinds of kangaroos (the 8 foot gray kangaroo and the small red one) and a few ostriches that could run 35 or 40 miles per hour.

Next I flew in a small plane over a great many big sheep and cattle ranches in what they call the Outback country. The guide told me that Australian sheep ranches produced more than a quarter of the world's wool.

The next morning I traveled to Ayers Rock. The guide said that I should see the big rock both at sunset and sunrise because it would appear in different colors. He was correct. The same small plane brought me back to Alice Springs where I saw a sheep shearing show.

I flew to Brisbane and went by bus to the Great Barrier Reef. I went out on a glass-bottom motor boat to see the very beautiful colored coral formations.

From there I went to Port Moresby, New Guinea and visited the wild natives of the island. The guide told me not to get into an argument with the natives because 8 years ago they had killed, cooked and eaten a missionary. The natives showed me a burial cave full of skeletons. These natives put on quite a different show for me. One performer put a live mouse in his mouth, chewed it up and swallowed it. Another show was called the Mud Dance in which 10 to 12 performers covered their bodies with white mud and went through various dances. When dressed in their native costumes, most of these shows were very colorful. The children, up to 8 years of age, were completely naked.

In New Guinea I saw two or three wrecked World War II Japanese planes in the jungle. At another place I stopped at a Japanese cemetery where they had buried their war dead. They had placed a wood Japanese shrine in the cemetery. The guide said most of the bodies had now been removed and taken back to Japan.

Then I took a plane back down to Sydney and flew to the Fiji Islands and Tahiti, the "Paradise of the Pacific." After a short stay, I boarded a plane for home.

In 1975 my next and last foreign trip was a 28 day trip to Norway, Sweden, Finland, The Soviet Union (Russia), and Germany. I flew to Oslo, Norway and saw the midnight sun. I looked out the second floor window of my hotel at midnight and saw that it was still twilight or more than half daylight outside. The cars moving on the street had only parking lights turned on.

The next morning the guide gave me a tour of Oslo. The Norwegians had always been seafaring people, and it seemed that most of their statues and memorials were related to the sea. In Frogner Park there were 150 nude statutes by one of Norway's greatest sculptors.

After a tour bus ride to Stockholm, Sweden, I visited a museum which had many artifacts concerning the sea. One outstanding display was a 400 year old wooden Viking battle ship which had been recovered from the bottom of the harbor. It was highly decorated with wooden carvings.

Next I visited Leningrad, Russia. Everything seemed to be highly guarded for tourists. The Russian guide took me on a tour of the Palace of the Czars which had been turned into a museum containing things which had belonged to the royal families back to around 1703. This museum, The Hermitage, had a lot of famous masterpieces of art.

I took a tour bus from Leningrad to Moscow. The guide checked me into a big tourist's hotel, which kept my passport until I left Moscow. That evening I decided to walk a few blocks from the hotel to a small fair with a giant ferris wheel. The people were all very well disciplined, and the teenagers acted more like adults. The public restroom was very clean.

The next morning I had to get up very early because the guide wanted to take me to Lenin's Tomb in Red Square. When I arrived, there was already a line of people 2 blocks long. Uniformed guards stood on each side of the tomb door. It was like walking into a refrigerator. I walked down a few steps and there was Lenin in a glass-topped casket. He looked like pink plastic.

After Joseph Stalin died in 1953, they put him in this tomb with Lenin but did not leave him there very long. They placed Stalin in a grave in the ground between the tomb and the Kremlin Wall where other statesmen were buried. Outside the Kremlin wall was the grave of U.S.S.R.'s Unknown Soldier.

Also in Red Square I viewed the famous St. Basil's Cathedral with its onion-shaped domes, built by Peter the Great. I thought it was badly in need of paint.

The next forenoon I once again took a city bus to Red Square for a tour inside the Kremlin. A tour like this was unheard of in the days of Stalin. The only building I was able to tour was the National Museum. I saw the early Czars' elaborate harnesses, really heavy and large royal coaches, one sleigh, pieces of furniture, dinnerware, and clothing.

I traveled by bus to Kiev, Ukraine which had the best farmland in all of Russia. The local guide showed me a very large memorial and mass graves of Russian soldiers either killed in fighting the Germans or murdered by them. People were still bringing flowers to these graves. This was a very sad place.

Next I went by bus to West Berlin and visited the ruins of the Kaiser Wilhelm Memorial Church which had been preserved as a grim reminder of the war. At the Berlin Wall, a platform had been built up on the west side so tourists could take a picture of an unmarked grass-covered mound (all that remained of the bunker where Hitler died). I saw the old Reichstag Government Building which had not been restored and the Brandenburg Gate which had been restored by the people of East Berlin.

The next morning the West Berlin tour guide took me to East Berlin. I arrived at the "Check-Point-Charlie" gate through the Berlin Wall. The guide turned me over to an East Berlin guide. Then the new guide took about 4 minutes comparing my passport photograph to me. While this was going on, 3 or 4 East German guards were outside with long handled mirrors looking under the bus. They even raised the hood over the motor. The new guide said I could keep my camera but she would tell me when I could start using it. One of the ladies on the tour said to me, "It's sure a good thing that

I happened to be wearing the same wig today that I was wearing in my passport photo, or I never would have made it through to East Berlin."

The bus drove past a lot of big buildings that were still in ruins. Some had been factories. Weeds and grass were growing on the windowsills. The guide told me I could use my camera. She showed us some big new apartment houses for working families and a few new small business places. Next she showed us what had been a very large church, The Berlin Church which was about half restored. Next we were taken to a very large and well maintained cemetery where a mass grave contained the Russian soldiers killed in the Battle for Berlin.

I noticed how few people and cars were on the East Berlin streets. This was sort of a weird tour, and I was glad to go west back through "Check-Point-Charlie."

The next morning I boarded a big plane for home.

Sharing My Trips and the Doll Collection

I carried two cameras on all six of my foreign trips. I took from 700 to 1,100 color slides on each trip and narrated them onto tape. After each trip, I showed them to the elementary students in the little gymnasium. Then for the next year or so, I would show the slides to various social groups in Mechanicsburg and to some nursing homes.

I collected 49 small handmade dolls with each one wearing handmade, native clothing. Those 49 dolls represented only about 35 different foreign countries because some were man and wife from one country. Both dolls and case were donated to the Mechanicsburg Public Library.

94

The Champaign County Bicentennial Capsule

Carl Coffey was the original chairman of the Bicentennial Capsule Committee, but he turned the whole project over to me. The capsule was for all of Champaign County because the 1976 school addition was the only new public building that was built in Champaign County that year. The Mechanicsburg Board of Education approved the capsule project. They ordered a heavy iron vault and then got 6 heavy cardboard boxes made that just fit in the iron vault. Cable, Christiansburg, Mechanicsburg/Goshen Township, North Lewisburg, St. Paris, and Urbana had one of the boxes for placing their time capsule items.

The vault was placed on a foundation of cement blocks under the stairway to your left as you entered the 1976 addition. The vault was sealed with an iron plate fastened with 6 heavy bolts. The bronze cover was in memory of Howard Moore, who donated the floodlights for the first Mechanicsburg football field.

Retirement

I really began to worry if I could still live without working at the school. I went to two fortune tellers: one in Springfield and one in Marysville. Both of them told me the same two things:

- After retirement I would find something very interesting to do, but I shouldn't expect any pay or salary for it.
- At one time in my life, I was very close to death.

I didn't understand the statement about death, because I had never been seriously sick nor in an accident. Maybe it was when the German sniper was shooting directly at me on the station platform. Or it could have been when we were crossing the North Atlantic on a greatly crowded troop ship, and the captain navigator had located a German submarine and zigzagged to get out of the German's gun sights. Another time may have been the night or two I spent in a foxhole on the Allied line in during the battle at Metz.

I really had planned to retire in 1976, but Superintendent Edward Everhart talked me into staying one more year. I was still in very good health and had missed only 3 days in 38 years, that being for Dad's funeral in 1967.

When I retired in July 1977, the curriculum was much broader than when I first came to Mechanicsburg in 1949. The textbooks and furniture were all up-to-date, and there was a much closer relationship between the school and community. The school had added 3 additions which provided a lot more space for both the elementary and high school students. The football field was much better. I had always had very good cooperation with the 9 superintendents and board members during my 28 years as principal.

The same Spring that I retired, the Mechanicsburg Lions Club selected me as the 1977 Man of the Year, an annual honor bestowed upon a selected citizen of Mechanicsburg or the community.

That same year, the Board of Education renamed and dedicated the Mechanicsburg Elementary School as the Dohron Wilson Elementary School. Dr. Everhart, Superintendent, and Virgil Rader, the Industrial Arts Teacher, constructed an antique fireplace and chimney in the front hall of the 1894 building. The Mechanicsburg Parent-Teacher Association arranged to have a large framed photograph of me placed on that brick chimney.

Champaign County Historical Museum

I was a life-long member and one of the trustees of the Champaign County Historical Society since it began in the present building. When the museum first moved into the building, I was asked to set up a display showing the interior of a one-room country school. Since then, 3 additions to the original building were constructed. I donated around 161 artifacts or antiques to the museum.

Before my parents' home sale in 1967, my sister and I decided to give the museum a lot of Dad's old 1916 horse-drawn farm machinery which was placed in the barn section of the museum along with my old 1937 Ford car.

In the main building, a 9 foot glass display case contained many World War II souvenirs that I picked up on battlefields in Europe.

The Eight Plaques in 1985

The awareness of Mechanicsburg's rich history was fading with the passing of one generation after another. I thought that a bronze plaque should be placed at important sites. I had the first one made for the hotel as example. Then I met with 7 various social groups in town, showed them the hotel plaque and asked them what they thought about purchasing a plaque for a historic building or site in town. All 7 groups agreed to purchase a plaque at $140 each.

Plaques were purchased and mounted (with the help of Charles Violet) at the hotel, the Hunt House on E. Sandusky Street, the Second Baptist Church, Site of the Old Town Hall, Site of the Town Pump in front of the Farmer's Bank, Site of the World War I Monument in the square, the oldest business building still being used, and the Central Ohio Fairgrounds.

99

OLDEST CHURCH IN
MECHANICSBURG

CONSTRUCTED, 1858

SITE OF THE
OLD TOWN HALL
1878 - 1972

PLAQUE PLACED BY THE MECHANICSBURG TOWN CLUB 1988

SITE OF OLD TOWN
DRINKING WATER PUMP
REMOVED, 1934

PLAQUE PLACED BY THE FAMILY OF W. W. McCOY, 1988

CENTER OF INTERSECTION
SITE OF WORLD WAR I
VETERANS MONUMENT, 1919-1934

PLAQUE PLACED BY DONALD CONRAD POST NO.239 OF AMERICAN LEGION

LAWLER'S TAVERN

OLDEST ORIGINAL BUSINESS
BUILDING IN MECHANICSBURG

CIRCA 1830

SITE OF
CENTRAL OHIO FAIR 1869-1896
MECH. CHAUTAUQUA 1910-1932
GOSHEN TWP. MEMORIAL PARK
DEDICATED 1948

ROBERT BUNYAN
PLAQUE PLACED BY PARK BOARD 1963; WAITE KELLER
WILLIAM SLIDDON

The 3 Year National Register Project

The Mechanicsburg Town Council employed the Benjamin Rickey Company of Columbus to investigate the history of selected sites in order to get the buildings and sites on the National Register in Washington D.C. I told the council I would help for no pay. The council voted $2,000 for the project, and the company got a federal grant of $4,000.

The next week I received my assignment which was to look up all courthouse records and conduct interviews with any senior citizens in town with historical information on 64 identified buildings. For the next two years, I spent most afternoons in the Champaign County Recorder's Office or talking to older citizens. All the information that I gathered was typed up and sent to the company.

In the meantime, the Benjamin Rickey Company came to Mechanicsburg and took a lot of photographs. After all this work, the company representative came back to Mechanicsburg and selected 24 buildings out of the original 64 to be nominated for Washington D.C.'s National Register of Historical Sites. Even though the Benjamin Rickey Company made the selection for the nominees, I did make sure that 7 or 8 sites were on their list. A letter asking for approval of a nomination was sent to each of the 24 owners before the nominations were mailed to Washington. If the owners did not want the nomination, then they had to reply that they objected. None replied, and the 24 sites were entered on the National Register; however, there were no government plaques awarded.

The Hunt home on East Sandusky was the most outstanding of the 24 nominations. The structure was still almost like it was in 1860. It was used to house slaves as part of the Underground Railroad and had a connection to the famous Addison White episode.

The hotel was constructed on the exact site of the first log and frame structure in Mechanicsburg. This new brick hotel was dedicated with much fanfare on December 31, 1875 with the name, Darby House. The entire second floor housed a public dining room and a large "gay nineties" ballroom. It was later known as the Anderson Inn of Mechanicsburg. After 120 years, it still is used for housing and has a restaurant on the first floor.

This building is on the site of the very first store in Mechanicsburg which could have been made of logs by John Owens. The present building often served as a grocery store. It was owned and operated by various grocery men such as: Mr. Culbertson, Ware & Culbertson, Ellis Boulton, and Gannons. It later became Michael's Dry Goods Store, Anderson's Clothing Store, and Spanger's Flowerland.

This building was constructed in 1877. Around 1900 Orla Shaw had a drug store in this building. Later, Mr. Newman had a small restaurant. For many years it has served as the barbershop with Don's Barbershop located there now.

In the 1900s, John Leidy had a candy kitchen and ice cream parlor in this building for many years. Around 1918, this building was occupied by a beer joint. Lately, the building has housed various beauty shops. Marcer's Beauty Salon is the current resident.

This is the original, small business building constructed soon after the close of the Civil War. Occupants of the building have been John Brinnon's meat shop, The Trader's Bank in 1894, Schetter's Jewelry Store, and now The Village Hobby Shop.

103

Lawler's Tavern is the oldest, original building still in use today. It was constructed by Dr. Lawler very close to 1830. It was the showplace on Main Street in 1840. The building was something like the early taverns along The Old National Pike (Route 40), only smaller. The doctor kept overnight lodgers on the second floor and lived and had his medical office on the first floor. It has since served as Miller Insurance and several doctors' offices.

This is Lot No. 77 and original No. 61 on the Putman's Addition laid out March15, 1836. This lot was sold by Isaac Putman on Feb. 8, 1836, to E.D. Lawler. This house was almost exactly like the old Underground Railroad Station House on the corner of E. Sandusky and Locust St. The same design, pattern and gingerbread trim were used on both houses. It was a very moderate home with a hand-hewed frame. Henry Burnham lived here. Then for many years, the building housed Dr. Ream's office.

The Magruder Building was originally constructed by Percy Moore in 1875. Magruder's Harness Shop was on the south side of the building, and Moore's Dry Goods Store was on the north side. There were insurance agencies on the second floor. The building has since housed Hennigan's Market, Smitty's Drug Store, pizza shops, and Saxbe's Law Office.

Robert Jones, who was the first owner of this lot, purchased it on March 10, 1849. It served many uses but was mainly grocery stores or carry-outs. Ralph Hamer operated the store for 23 years. It had always been a typical country store where the business stayed open odd hours and ran a cash business.

The charter for the Clinton Lodge No. 113 Free and Accepted Masons was granted in 1843. They met in various halls until their first assembly room was provided in the old M.P. Church in 1855. They had to move from there in 1889 because a new church was to be constructed on that site. The Lodge meetings were moved to the second floor of the old Central Bank located in the Taylor Building on S. Main. They met at this location until 1909 when they completed the present, beautiful and commodious Masonic Temple.

This is Lot No. 27 of the original town plat laid out August 6, 1814. It was owned by John Kain, Richard Lansdale, and the trustees of the M.E. Church before it was sold to Annie Ninchelser. Annie, the new wife of Dr. Oram Ninchelser, was from New York City and liked to display her social standing. In order to keep her in Mechanicsburg, Dr. Ninchelser built the present very fine brick residence. They lived together in the residence for a few years until Annie divorced the doctor and moved back to a more desirable "city" social life. A few years later Dr. Ninchelser sold the house to The Wildey Lodge 271 (I.O.O.F.). The Odd Fellow Lodge now owns this town "show piece."

This church is on Lot No. 45 and the original No. 29 of the Putman's Addition which was laid out on March 15, 1836. The various owners were John Kain, Richard Lansdale, and Thomas Glendening. The Trustees of the M.E. Church purchased the land on August 18, 1893. The church was constructed and dedicated in April 1894. The Methodist congregation began in 1814 in a combination log building used for both school and church. It was located to the rear of the present Second Baptist Church. In 1819, they built a separate frame church just to the east. The very first cemetery was also started just east of the 1819 church. In 1839, the Methodists built and moved to a church at the corner of Locust and E. Sandusky. They then constructed the 1858 church (now the Second Baptist Church). Finally, they built the present church on E. Race and N. Main.

The Episcopal Church was first organized in July 1892. Their first meetings were held in the Town Hall. The present church lot was purchased in 1893 for a sum of $1,000 with church construction totaling $5,000. On December 10, 1893, the dedication services were held in the church. Social meeting rooms were added over the past years.

St. Michael Parish group was first organized in 1865 and was ministered by Father Kearney of St. Mary's Church in Urbana until 1871. Eventually, a pastor was assigned to Immaculate Conception (North Lewisburg) and St. Michael's. The present church on Walnut St. was constructed in 1886.

This church was situated on the exact site of the first church that the Methodist Protestant congregation built after splitting from the Methodist church on E. Sandusky over the issue of slavery. During the summer of 1890, the old 1853 church was torn down with the dedication of the new building being held on February 15, 1891. The church was sold to the Baptist congregation in 1956.

The Second Baptist Church is in the oldest continuously used church building in Mechanicsburg. The building had previously been the M.E. Church.

This property on Lot No. 22 was owned by John Kain, John Owens, Richard Lansdale, and Andrew Staley. The most famous owner of the house was Levi Rathburn, the operator of an Underground Railroad Station. Throughout the years, the home retained its look from the mid 1800s.

This house was owned by William Culbertson, the owner of Culbertson Buggy Works

Cyrus Barr, a blacksmith and part owner of the Culbertson Buggy Works, lived in this residence at the corner of Locust and E. Race Streets.

This fine old brick home was on the north part of Lot No. 3 of the original plat. Dr. Clark, a prominent medical doctor, lived here and built a little room attached to the Lawler Tavern for his office. Other residents included the Tullis and Miller families.

This property was owned by John Kain, John Thompson, and Neil Gest. Dr. Demand, a local medical doctor, built the present house around 1900. It was built when wealthy neighbors were trying to out-build their neighbors.

Elias Keys, Charles Dresser, J.P. Taylor, and J.F. Kimball owned this property. John Kimball, a very wealthy farmer, had the present home built in 1897 to out-rank any of his neighbors.

Major John Baker had this 1863 home constructed on the exact site of John Kain's original double log cabin. The Wing family resided in this house for many years.

Mr. Horr built the Hunter brick house in 1850. The first Hunter family moved here from Virginia in 1863. The house was extensively remodeled in 1910. The house and the farm have been in the Hunter family for over 130 years.

Other Significant Activities

Since retiring in 1977, Elizabeth Ball and Sue Marsh organized an annual birthday party for me in the school cafeteria. Sue always baked and decorated a large cake for me  and had other cakes cut into smaller pieces for each elementary student. The students made many homemade birthday cards. I greatly appreciated these efforts of Elizabeth, Sue and the kids.

I had furnished and operated a public address system for the Mechanicsburg Arts and Crafts Festival since it started. We used to use Lowell Tullis's 40 foot trailer as a stage across Main Street which I decorated. This was a lot easier after the festival was moved to the park.

I wrote 8 to 10 little booklets on individual historical subjects in and around Mechanicsburg. These were filed in the Mechanicsburg Public Library.

I held a life membership with three organizations: The Champaign County Historical Society, The Ohio Retired Teachers' Association, and the Veterans of Foreign Wars Association.

During the Masonic Lodges' combined 1992 annual meeting in London, consisting of Madison, Union, Clark, and Champaign Counties, the members awarded me their Community Service Award. I felt very honored to have been nominated by the Mechanicsburg Masons and awarded this large attractive award.

A Great Life

Since my September 1949 arrival in Mechanicsburg, I became a part of the school and community. I greatly enjoyed every minute of the experience. The whole community and school had been so cooperative. Now, at a little past 81 years of age, I'm slowing down.

All the Mechanicsburg school children that were born between 1937 and 1972 had me as an elementary principal. (The 6th grade kids were already 12 years old when I came in 1949. The 5 year old kindergarten kids that I had in 1977 were born in 1972.)

So I have had hundreds of children and have seen their kids grow up and begin professions and jobs of their own. I feel blessed to have had the opportunity to be a part of the community and to make it a better place for our future generations. For this I am grateful!

Postscript

Mr. Wilson remained in the Champaign County Nursing Home, and over time his health continued to fail. On occasion he was referred to the hospital for health reasons but was under the nursing home's care. From time to time, I would go to Columbus and pick up Geneva McCormick, Mr. Wilson's sister, and we would go visit him.

Mr. Wilson was transferred to Springfield for care. On May 17, 1995, I got a call that he was not doing well, and family should come quickly. I made a fast trip to Columbus to pick up Mrs. McCormick, and then we traveled to St. John's Nursing Center in Springfield. When we arrived on the second floor, the charge nurse met us at the elevator and advised us that Mr. Wilson had passed 30 minutes earlier.

Mr. Wilson was gone, and our community had lost a great and dedicated man.

Many of his "kids" and community members attended his funeral service. The ole school bell sounded its final "good-bye" as his cortege paused in front of the school on its way to Maple Grove Cemetery.

-Don Hunt

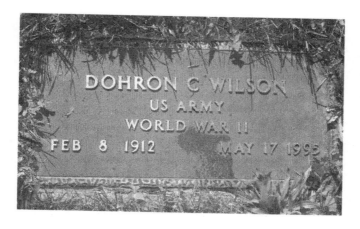

WILSON
DOHRON C.
1912 — 1995

OHIO
TEC. 4 Co. D 378 INF. REGT. 95TH DIV.
U.S. ARMY   WORLD WAR II

EDUCATOR

114

Addendum

1992 Community Service Award Nomination

Dohron C. Wilson is nominated for the Community Service Award for his continued involvement and giving to the community of Mechanicsburg and Champaign County over the past 43 years. He is a dedicated, involved individual who has given his full life to the community, its people, and its history. As an educator with the local school system for 28 years, his influence has affected generations. He is a man of the community that very much exemplifies the "True Spirit of Freemasonry".

Mr. Wilson was born February 8, 1912 and graduated from Dexter City High School in 1931. He attended Ohio University and obtained a two year teaching certificate and began teaching in Jackson Township Schools in 1933 where he stayed for 9 years. He joined the US Army in July 1942, served three years in the European Theater, earned the Bronze Star in the battle of Metz and separated from the military in November 1945. He reentered Ohio University, obtained his Bachelor of Science in Education and began work on a Master's Degree. He taught school in the Fairfield County school system for one year and in 1949 entered the Mechanicsburg School System as the Elementary Principal serving until retirement in 1977. He completed his Master's Degree in 1954.

Mr. Wilson has been active in school and community affairs since his arrival in 1949. Early on, he took personal interest in the elementary school, the teachers, students and all activities. He made education interesting and fun. He got people involved with projects, displays, parades, plays, the PTA, field trips and contests all designed to complement the learning experience. His Christmas display in the Elementary School each year was a special project that he personally did.

Each year he would locate a 15 foot Christmas tree, cut it, set up and decorate the tree along with a family Christmas display. Every year, because of Mr. Wilson's efforts, Santa would visit the school with a small fruit and cookie gift for each elementary student. In later years, Mr. Wilson, out of his own funds, purchased a very large artificial tree for the school so the tradition which he had started could be carried on after he was gone.

The school children were always important to Mr. Wilson and he always made sure they were taken care of whenever there was a need. When he found that children frequently got wet and muddy at recess, he worked with the school room mothers who donated children's clothes to the school. Mr. Wilson bought a washer and dryer for the school with his own funds. When a student got wet or muddy at recess, Mr. Wilson made sure the student had clean dry clothes, washed the student's clothes during the day so the student could go home with the same clean dry clothes they came to school with.

Mr. Wilson's love for "his kids" and the school was further demonstrated when he bought a large wooden Indian for the school with his own funds. Out of his own pocket he purchased a portable public address system to meet all the school's needs. Whether it was a pet parade or a pep rally, Mr. Wilson was a force that gave life to it. He was the leader and orchestrator in attending to the many details that made a function happen.

In the late 1960's and early 1970's, Mr. Wilson traveled six summers to places all over the world. He returned with hundreds of slides, souvenirs and material from places he had visited. He built his experiences into "talks" for the school, the Tourist Club, the Lion's Club, church groups and other community groups. As part of his travels, he built a collection of dolls from 49 countries around the world dressed in their

116

native clothes. He donated the collection to the village library and purchased a trophy case to display the dolls, identifying each doll and its country.

Mr. Wilson's achievements and contributions to the school are almost too numerous to mention. He was dedicated to the school and "his kids". In 1977, after 28 years as the Elementary Principal, Mr. Wilson retired. In May of 1977. Mechanicsburg selected Dohron Wilson for the community's prestigious award of "Man of the Year". At the same time, the Mechanicsburg Elementary School was formally renamed the Dohron Wilson Elementary School in honor of all that Mr. Wilson had done and given to the school and community over his 28 years.

Formal retirement was only a "pause" for Mr. Wilson. He remained very active and involved in the community. His first act was to purchase and donate a spiral slide to the elementary school with the severance money he was given at retirement.

Mr. Wilson, a historian, placed his energies into the village and county histories. As a charter member and trustee of the Champaign County Historical Society, he devoted his efforts to supplying and developing the county historical museum into one of the best, most well-furnished county museums in Ohio. He began a drive to place several Mechanicsburg buildings on the National Register with the Department of Interior as historical facilities. He researched 64 sites and of these, *24* were accepted to the National Registry. This three year project from 1983 to 1985 was not just an individual effort; it was a community project that stirred the interest of the village. By talking with ladies' clubs, churches and other various groups the project was accomplished because of Mr. Wilson's interest and involvement. As a follow-up effort, Mr. Wilson saw that eight of the key sites selected had a bronze plaque located on the facility. Since the village was a major stopover and important part of the Underground Railway System of the Civil War, Mr. Wilson spent much time developing, preserving and writing about its history in Mechanicsburg. He authored articles for the library and newspapers, had interviews on TV and made people aware of the history that existed. In researching the slave history and Underground Railway System, Mr. Wilson discovered that two famous slaves of the village were buried in the town cemetery but had no headstone marker. Mr. Wilson purchased headstones and had the graves properly marked

When the town began its annual Arts Festival at the town park, Mr. Wilson became one of the key people in making it a successful event. He helped by arranging and preparing the public address system and by giving support to all the various participating agencies. He had personal interest and involvement in every Memorial Day service. He helped arrange activities, set up services, was a participant in wreath laying, provided a P.A. system and he marched in his World War II uniform.

Mr. Wilson has commissioned paintings at his expense of two historical facilities in the community. He has authored several articles on the community and things of significance. All are on file in the town library. Mr. Wilson holds three permanent Ohio teaching certificates. He is a life member of the Ohio Retired Teachers Association. He is also a life member and trustee of the Champaign Historical Society and he is a member of the Veterans of Foreign Wars.

Dohron Wilson is a man of the community. He's involved, dedicated, active and committed to the community. He has given his life effort to the school and community in making it a better place to live. Mechanicsburg and the community are better off because of Mr. Wilson's contributions. He has touched everyone's life directly or indirectly because of his life and love of the community. He has given of himself in a way that exemplifies the "True Spirit of Freemasonry" and makes him most worthy for the community service award.

Remembering Mr. Wilson

Our growing-up years were typical of all farm kids. We had chores to do. Dad was a sheep farmer. When a sheep refused to mother her lamb, Dohron and I fed them and raised them by hand. I can hear Mom being upset when one of our pets got into the yard and ate the leaves of her rose bushes. Dad never sold these lambs at market time. They lived on the farm till old age took them. At shearing time we were right there when our pets were sheared, when Dad weighed their fleeces and when the fleeces sold. Dohron and I got the money for the fleeces in our banks. We didn't know it then, but Mom and Dad were teaching us several good things.

In the 20's when we didn't have a car, Dad borrowed Grandpa's surrey with the fringe on top, and we made a trip to Caldwell twice a year. Mom wanted pictures taken during our growing years so that meant getting dressed up which Dohron didn't like. He preferred his bib overalls. Also, he said that I grinned too much in the pictures. So things got a bit hectic on picture day. On the way to town, I'd get some elbow jabs when Mom wasn't looking.

Grandfather Webber was always there for us. He had a Model T Ford and took Dohron and me to the circus, county fairs and picnics. He bought us our first phonograph. We loved him so much.

Grandfather gave us a wooden wagon for a Christmas present. Back then the country roads weren't paved and were too muddy even for a horse and buggy sometimes. That was the situation when he wanted to bring the wagon to us for Christmas. So he rigged up a sled-like thing, put the wagon on it, and pulled it across the fields from his house to ours so we'd have the wagon for Christmas. When we outgrew the wagon, it was roped up in the rafters of the barn where it stayed for many years.

When Mom needed something from the Crooked Tree General Store, she would send us with three dozen eggs in a basket to get it. The barter system was used. The eggs might bring $.15 a dozen making $.45 which bought what we came to get. On these trips we had a nickel to spend for ourselves. Our Uncle Clifford owned the store, and he always gave us six penny sticks of peppermint candy for our nickel. He always cut a piece of cheese from the big wheel of cheese for us to eat on our walk home.

There was a big pot-bellied stove in the middle of the store where in winter the neighborhood men gathered to smoke their pipes and discuss everything from politics to gossip. They were called loafers.

The accumulation of smells in a general store can't be found anywhere else: freshly ground coffee beans, big wheel of cheese, all kinds of spices, yard goods, and pipe smoke from the loafers.

Uncle Clifford and his store were special to us. Dohron's middle name was Clifford for Uncle Clifford, Mom's brother.

When Dohron was old enough, Dad bought him a gun. Squirrels and groundhogs were about his limit. I didn't like hunting and guns. I would go to school a half hour early so I wouldn't hear the gun shots on our annual pig butchering day.

121

One Sunday I'd been at Sunday school. I came home and something smelled good. Dohron said it was chicken. I ate it, and then he told me I had just eaten squirrel that he had shot that morning. I didn't forgive him for a long time. I don't know why Mom let him get away with that deception.

In 1929 the crash came and the depression started. The banks failed and only one returned any money, and that was $.15 on the dollar. That was where Dohron's college money was. He graduated high school in the spring of 1930. Dad hadn't sold his wool yet but the price per pound for wool was almost down to nothing.

Our mom was a school teacher from 1902-1910, and she valued education. She was determined that what was needed would be there when college started in the fall for Dohron; and it was. The money from the wool helped the college fund. So along with other savings, there was enough for Dohron to start Ohio University in the fall. With Mom's regular care boxes of bread, cookies, and a jar of her cold-packed beef, all went well for Dohron.

-Geneva Wilson McCormick
Mr. Wilson's sister

Mr. Wilson was part of my life for 46 years, and as the years passed the relationship changed from little boy's principal to adult's close friend. But he was always "Mr. Wilson" to me. I don't recall of ever addressing him as Dohron. It was just something I never did or thought of doing.

Mr. Wilson had a high energy level and was always "going" even in his late stages of his life. He stayed busy and was always working on some kind of a project for the school, library, museum, community, or some other organization. He was always committed to the task at hand.

Mr. Wilson was shy and at times withdrawn. This wasn't the case if he was making a talk or presentation to a group. Then he was in his arena where he felt comfortable.

He had a good sense of humor, but it was guarded and unfortunately it didn't come out enough.

Mr. Wilson held his emotions in check, except there were times when he could show some anger and displeasure at a situation. I saw Mr. Wilson cry twice in my life which was a part of the man I had never seen before. In 1968 when my father died and in 1992 when my wife passed, he wept as we all were in my mom's kitchen. He was close to both Dad and Nancy, and he was visibly hurt.

-Don Hunt
MHS Class of 1959

I first met Dohron Wilson when I was in the first grade in 1949. He was a very quiet and stern principal. The next time that his presence was significant in my life was when I was living at 106 North Main Street in Mechanicsburg, Ohio. Our family was going to be moving up the street to 139 North Main. Dohron was renting a room at the house we were moving to. Prior to moving up the street, Dohron came to talk with my father to find out whether he could continue renting his room or would have to move out. This was not known to my brother and me. All we knew was the principal of our school was meeting with our parents, and we didn't think we'd done anything wrong. The mystery of this meeting defined Dohron Wilson. He was a very quiet, caring and sensitive person.

The Hunt family moved to 139 North Main Street, and Dohron kept renting a room there with the Hunt family. Dohron became part of the family. He came to our dinner table for Thanksgiving and Christmas holidays always arriving just before we were about to eat. In his quiet way, he would be a very nice, pleasant person.

The first surprising experience of living with Dohron was when he played "Turkey in the Straw." If you don't know the song, it is a knee slapping song. Dohron played the song on an old 78 RPM record. My brother and I heard it, and we were getting a kick out of the "quiet man" playing such lively music. We told him to turn it up louder so we could hear it too.

I think the underlying relationship was that my brother and I were just being one of Mr. Wilson's "kids." Mr. Wilson had many boys and girls that he loved. He cared for them by cleaning up scratched knees from the playground, decorating the school for Christmas, buying playground equipment from his own pocket, and even giving a paddling to a student who needed disciplining. However, the biggest impact was his caring for the children to become good citizens.

I remember Dohron going up the stairs to his room at the house. He would take two steps at a time. As I think about this now, I think that he took two steps at a time because he was in a hurry. He had many things to do.

I had a very memorable, personal experience with Mr. Wilson during his sixth grade history class. Mr. Wilson was the grade school principal and also taught sixth grade history.

Mr. Wilson's method of teaching history was to lecture about a few pages from our history book that we should have read. Mr. Wilson loved history so much that his lectures were, for the most part, very interesting and entertaining. During one class in 1955 I was not paying attention and whispering to everyone around me. Mr. Wilson had just enough of me not paying attention. He came back to my desk, grabbed me on my shoulders and shook me up and down. I stopped talking. He talked with my parents that night. I learned a lesson.

My final memory is traveling in Mr. Wilson's funeral procession, stopping by the old elementary building and hearing the school bell ring. The physical sound of the bell put thoughts in my mind of a great, caring and loving person.

The new grade school in Mechanicsburg now is referred to as Dohron Wilson Elementary. This gives me much pleasure, and I would like to think that Dohron is smiling too.

-Thomas W. Hunt
MHS Class of 1961

We lived beside Dohron Wilson for many years while he was elementary principal. He resided in an apartment in the home of Martha and Marion Hunt on N. Main St.

As neighbors we became fast friends as he watched our children grow up, tolerated our pets and loved my flower beds. He took pictures when the flowers were in full bloom, framed them with construction paper and presented them to me. He was a quiet man but was fast moving with coat tails flying as he headed for the school each day to take care of his flock.

I worked for the Board of Education. While we worked in separate buildings, I would occasionally pass him in the halls. Each time he would smile but not tarry while on his way somewhere! I know he was not only a family friend but honored me with a level of trust in handling the finances of the school. Many times we discussed the importance of being frugal while making sure the children were served. He trusted my office with important documents that needed to be preserved for the future, feeling that my office would be the "proper place."

Few knew that he had a sense of humor. He observed that I had a statue of St. Francis (patron saint of animals) in my flower garden. A storm knocked it over one day, and the head fell off. He came over and confronted me with the problem. In his wry way he asked, "Well, what are you going to do now?" I simply said, "Well, I am going to glue his head back on." He gave a chuckle and moved on.

Mr. Wilson would also question if my car knew its way "anywhere except to the school." His humor was quiet and swift, but you knew it was his "hand of friendship."

We all know there will never be another Mr. Wilson, and what a shame that is! Few know the wealth of experiences he brought to Mechanicsburg students from his travels as well as the security he afforded little children who feared him.

What a guy!

-Alice Creamer
Friend and neighbor

I have so many fond memories of Mr. Wilson beginning in elementary school when he was my history teacher and my principal. The stories he would tell and the way he would tell them made our history lessons come alive and easy to remember. Another part of my elementary experience that was easy to remember was the two whacks (more like gentle taps) he gave me for being on the front lawn of the school. This is when I first learned of his infamous paddle, the one he held up the sleeve of his jacket. He would enter our room, let the paddle slide down into his hand and slam it on a desk. He not only got our attention with this tactic

126

but also nearly scared us out of our seats. Whatever rule, behavior or point he wanted us to understand, we knew he meant business.

One of the early traditions he started, which the students loved, was "The Pet Parade." In late October, he would have whoever wanted to be in "The Pet Parade" dress up in his or her Halloween costume and bring their pet (who could also be dressed in a costume) to school. These students would then parade in a circle on the football field while the other students watched. A King and Queen were crowned, and everyone enjoyed all the activity that went on with the pets.

I'm sure everyone who had Mr. Wilson as a principal remembers, as I do, the huge Christmas tree that he decorated and placed outside his office. He also had a six foot mechanical Santa and a fireplace that he decorated for the occasion. The last day before Christmas break, he would have all the students gather around the tree and sing Christmas songs and carols. When they were dismissed, each child passed by Santa who then handed them a special Christmas treat. All of Mr. Wilson's Christmas preparations and activities filled everyone with the Christmas spirit.

It would take a book to tell all the things that Mr. Wilson's students remember about him. Everyone you talk with could share some special memory. These were just a few of mine when I was his student. I am so very glad that he chose Mechanicsburg and became my principal and my very dear friend. He will always be remembered for all that he did for our community, our school, and for the part he played in our lives.

Thank you, Mr. Wilson!
-Becky Ball

Mr. Wilson was a huge influence on me becoming an elementary school teacher and my style of teaching. I learned from him that teachers must make the subject matter interesting and engage the students in discussion. While I was at Ohio State, Mr. Wilson permitted me to come to school and help the teachers during the time in the fall before my classes started. This gave me some practical experience and counted toward fulfilling an OSU College of Education requirement called "September Experience". In later years when I came back to the Burg to visit my parents, he was always wanting to hear about my teaching career.

I was disciplined once in sixth grade but it made me respect him even more. I think that was his first or so year in the Burg. I have never forgotten the discipline and his influence on my life and career.

-Nancy R. Hunt Bullard

At Christmas time, the 1894 building was adorned with an automated, talking Santa which he had purchased and dressed in a new suit. The chimney was decorated to look like a fireplace with stockings hanging from the mantel. The huge Christmas tree filled the lobby. At recess, Mr. Wilson would have Christmas music "blaring" in the hallway. The students were so excited that last week before Christmas. It was difficult for the teachers to get the children to behave and complete school work. Trying to get anything done in the school office was almost an impossible task.

-Marilyn McIntire
Elementary School Secretary
(retold by her daughter, **Becky McIntire Babicz**))

I remember Mr. Wilson very fondly as the strong leader of Mechanicsburg Elementary School. You just knew he was in charge. Always attired properly, he gave the impression of what a principal should look like. It seems like he always wore a blue suit, white long sleeved shirt and a tie.

I remember he always took the stairs two at a time, seems that he was in a hurry to get to his destination. As students, we were always wary of his "wooden soldier" that we believed he carried up his sleeve. He used that to maintain a sense of decorum within the school and quickly "put the consequences of misconduct behind the errant student."

He had a wry sense of humor but was very approachable by students and parents. Like all good principals, he strongly supported his teachers. My guess is,

129

however, that on that rare occasion when a teacher needed some counseling, he was direct and firm in addressing them.

As a former principal myself, I look back at Mr. Wilson and view him as the role model of the dedicated principal who ran his school with a firm but understanding hand. He could be tough when the conditions warranted it, but could also be friendly and compassionate when needed. He is one that other principals could look to as an example of success. He understood that the school existed for the students, and he served his community well. Thousands of alumni can look back at their early years of schooling and count their lucky stars to have been blessed by his caring hand.

-Tom Rutan
MHS Class of 1961

One of my favorite memories of school was when principal, Dohron Wilson, filled in as a substitute teacher. He had a humorous down to earth style of teaching. History, he explained was merely "his story". Compound fractions were simply top heavy numbers that needed balance ($10/7 = 1\ 3/7$). He also said (I thought he looked directly at me) fancy clothes and rings on the fingers didn't mean there are brains in the head, and sometimes the poorest people have the most talent.

-Joan Rogers Krukewitt
MHS Class of 1961

In 1968 I became secretary at Mechanicsburg Exempted Village Schools. My duties were to manage the high school office and act as secretary to both the high school principal and the superintendent. After a few years, the high school principal's and superintendent's offices were separated into two individual offices. A new high school secretary was employed, and I became the administrative assistant to the

Superintendent. After twenty-five years of happy school employment, I retired.

Dohron Wilson was the elementary principal, and since there was no elementary secretary at the time he would sometimes ask me to type some of his correspondence. Even though the board of education employed an elementary secretary a few years later, Mr. Wilson made me feel special by still asking me to type some of his confidential correspondence and reports, such as teacher evaluations, which I was always happy to do.

Mr. Wilson was a very dedicated principal. The most important things in his life were his students and his teachers. He was a fair disciplinarian, respected by all of the school employees and loved by all the students.

-Louise Mohr Gossett

During my early Mechanicsburg Elementary days, I truly believed that Mr. Wilson lived at the school. He was always there: before school, after school, weekends, football games, and even during the summer.

In the summer, my friends and I often rode our bikes around the school and stopped to enjoy the playground equipment. I would always see Mr. Wilson dressed like I was not used to seeing him-in gray coveralls and a straw hat. He was painting or repairing the playground equipment. He wouldn't say much to us as he had too much work to do.

-Glenn Lewis

I don't think anyone from the "older" generation has a childhood memory of Mechanicsburg Elementary that doesn't include Mr. Wilson: be it his antique car in parades playing "Battle of New Orleans", the beautiful Christmas tree he put up in the elementary hallway, his cartoons at Christmas, slide shows of his trips, or him standing in the doorway as we came in at recess.

131

Mr. Wilson seemed to be a man of few words, and as we all know, a strict disciplinarian. Although he had no children of his own, he raised thousands. As children we did not see what he did for us was out of love.

My mom, Sue Marsh, and Aunt Becky Ball celebrated his birthday for several years with a party at school. My brother Gregg's birthday was the same day as Mr. Wilson's, and he always remembered to tell Gregg to have a great birthday.

A vivid memory of his caring and understanding was my mother's continuing problem of keeping my brother, Gregg, in school. Gregg was in the first grade and Mom worked in the cafeteria. Every day at recess (and at that time we had three), Gregg would go home. Mr. Wilson would go to the cafeteria and let Mom know Gregg had left again. Mom would drive home and find Gregg sitting on the porch. She would take him back to school. When the next recess came, Mr. Wilson would be back in the cafeteria to let Mom know he was gone again. This went on for several weeks. As we all know, you did not want to be sent to Mr. Wilson's office. It was to us, a death sentence. But everyday Mr. Wilson took Gregg to his office to talk to him, and try to convince him to stay at school. I am not sure what those talks were about, but Gregg seemed to enjoy them as they were almost a daily occurrence. It worked. After a couple weeks Gregg began to stay at school. Mr. Wilson could have had Gregg stay in at recess or tied him to his chair, but in this case, he knew that understanding and patience were the keys.

Even though, we as children did not understand Mr. Wilson's ways, as adults we see he cared for each of us. Perhaps, today's schools could all benefit from a little of Mr. Wilson and his ways. With fond memories,

-Hope Marsh Stout

One year Mr. Wilson showed up at the library with a small Christmas tree and some decorations that he had purchased. Miss Marion Bradley went to the basement and brought up a box of decorations that the library owned.

Miss Bradley and Mr. Wilson decided that the tree should be placed on top of a table in the back section of the library. There was much discussion about how the tree should be decorated. They decided to each decorate a side of the tree. As they began moving around the tree to decorate, Mr. Wilson took the decorations that Miss Bradley had hung and rehung them the way he wanted them. When she saw her decorations moved, she rehung them to where she thought they looked best. This went on for 45 minutes until Miss Bradley called an end to decorating.

After Mr. Wilson left the library, Miss Bradley went back and rehung the ornaments the way she wanted them hung.

-Mechanicsburg Public Library Staff

Mr. Wilson, our elementary principal, was a formidable presence. It really wasn't just because of his neat light gray-blue suits, intense blue eyes, straight posture, stern reprimands, or being the vigilant observer. When I was a child, I found him frightening at times. But, by the time I reached my teen years and came back to visit him for various reasons, I found myself seeing the "formidable" Mr. Wilson as someone I really admired and enjoyed.

I began to see a humble, kind-hearted man who was at peace with what his calling was. I saw him as a very dedicated educator. He was always on the lookout for opportunities to expand our world and make our memories of school special. He did the same for our community in his dedicated work to compile and preserve the little town of Mechanicsburg's history. He enriched our lives. In the end, he earned a small part of our hearts forever. The last time I saw him, I remember his smiling face, with the twinkle in his fading blue eyes and his words of encouragement. He saw something in me that for a long time I never saw. He helped me to believe in myself and that someday, I could make a difference in this world too. Thank you, Mr. Wilson.

-Nancy Brown Raley
Class of 1970

Mr. Wilson! Oh yes, I have many memories of this dear man. Many to share and some that will remain just a memory.

As a child, I lived on the same street as Mr. Wilson. I was amazed how fast he could walk down North Main Street to eat his evening meal. I would sit in Dad's chair just to watch Mr. Wilson pass by.

On my first day of first grade, I thought it was a good idea to watch the football team practice instead of going home. Mr. Wilson made it clear not to make this decision again.

One evening I thought I would take another way home. The patrol officer took me to the office for jay-walking. Mr. Wilson placed numerous paddles on his desk and warned me that if I ever jay-walked again, he would paddle me. I knew he would because I remember him walking the hallways with the paddle up his sleeve.

I will always remember Mr. Wilson playing the music at the football games and ringing the victory bell.

After completing college, I applied at Mechanicsburg Elementary. Mr. Hall, the superintendent, interviewed me and then asked Mr. Wilson to come to the office and interview me. I was quite nervous. The only thing Mr. Wilson said to me was that if I ever became pregnant he would never recommend me for another job.

Yes, he had trouble adjusting to the changing times. He finally allowed women teachers to wear pants!

Being efficient and timely were very important to Mr. Wilson. If teachers did not have their reports completed on time, he would announce their names during morning announcements for all students and teachers to hear.

A very special memory I have is the day of Mr. Wilson's funeral. My husband, Ed, and I rang the school's bell during the funeral procession for one of Mechanicsburg's finest.

-Peggy Moore Foulk

About the Producers

Don Hunt graduated from Mechanicsburg in 1959 and obtained a B.S. Business degree from Wittenberg University in 1963. He obtained a Master's Degree from Southern Illinois University and graduated from the Executive Business Course at the Kellogg School of Business, Northwestern University. Additionally, he graduated from military professional schools including Squadron Officer's School, Command and Staff School, and the Industrial College of the Armed Forces. He served 26 years with the United States Air Force. Don also has served as a substitute high school teacher, Sergeant-of-Arms of the Ohio Senate, and Director of Corporations for the Ohio Secretary of State. He was the first non-attorney to serve on the Unauthorized Practice of Law Board for the Ohio Supreme Court. He is now fully retired and helps local nursing homes with his AAT certified therapy dog. Don also enjoys recreational private flying.

Tom Hunt was born and raised in Mechanicsburg, Ohio and has always considered it his home. He lived at 139 North Main Street from 1952 to 1965. During those years Dohron Wilson (aka Mr. Wilson) rented a room from his parents. Tom, one of Mr. Wilson's many students, graduated from Mechanicsburg High School, Miami University (Oxford, Ohio) and received a master's in Mathematics teaching from Andrews University in Berrien Springs, Michigan. After teaching 4 years in Niles, Michigan, Tom went into the business world of helping people use computers. While working in the business world, Tom taught evening classes of computer programming and Mathematics at Kirtland Community College and Northwestern Michigan College. After 25 years, Tom retired from the business world and now enjoys swimming at the local YMCA along with all the other pleasures of retirement.

My brother, Don Hunt, had collected writings from Mr. Wilson while he was in the Champaign County Nursing Home. Don suggested to me that I use my computer skills, and we could work together and produce a book about Mr. Wilson. This project has been in the making for the last 2 years with various starts and stops, but it has not lacked the enthusiasm of wanting to tell the story. Mr. Dohron Wilson was a very remarkable person whose love was teaching children. Assisting in putting this book together has been a labor of love. I hope the reader sees the goodness this educator did for Mechanicsburg.

Glenn Lewis, one of Mr. Wilson's "kids," graduated from Mechanicsburg High School in 1969. He received a B.S. in Elementary Education from Urbana College in 1973, and a dual masters in Curriculum/Supervision and Administration from Wright State University. Glenn worked 32 years in the Graham Local School District as a classroom teacher, a special reading teacher, an elementary principal, and a Transportation Supervisor. Upon retirement, he taught Early Childhood Education courses for the Education Department of Urbana University and briefly served as Director of Teacher Education. Glenn currently is involved with numerous volunteer activities.

Acknowledgements

The Producers are indebted to The Champaign County Historical Museum and The Mechanicsburg Public Library for contributing valuable information and photographs to this book.